From Famine to Feast

Economic and Social Change in Ireland
1847–1997

RTÉ Thomas Davis Lecture Series: Winter 1997/98

From Famine to Feast

Economic and Social Change in Ireland 1847–1997

Lectures on the occasion of the 150th anniversary of the Statistical and Social Inquiry Society of Ireland

General Editor: Michael Littleton
Consulting Editor: Kieran A. Kennedy

IPA
INSTITUTE OF PUBLIC ADMINISTRATION

First published in 1998
by the
Institute of Public Administration
57–61 Lansdowne Road
Dublin 4
Ireland

British Library Cataloguing in Publication Data
A catalogue record for this book is available from the British Library

The Thomas Davis Lectures
General Editor: Michael Littleton

Every autumn, winter and spring since September 1953, Radio Telefis Éireann has been broadcasting half-hour lectures, named in honour of Thomas Davis. Inspired by one of his famous sayings, 'Educate that you may be free', the aim of these lectures has been to provide in popular form what is best in Irish scholarship and the sciences.

The Winter 1997/98 series was organised on the occasion of the 150th anniversary of the Statistical and Social Inquiry Society of Ireland, the Consulting Editor for the series being Kieran A. Kennedy, a past president of the Society. The lectures were delivered weekly on RTÉ Radio 1, starting on Monday 17 September 1997 and finishing on Monday 16 February 1998.

ISBN 1 902448 03 0

Typeset in 11/12 Times New Roman by the Institute of Public Administration, Dublin
Printed by ColourBooks Ltd, Dublin

Contents

Contributors

Mary Daly is Associate Professor of Modern Irish History at University College Dublin

Cormac Ó Gráda is Associate Professor of Economic History at University College Dublin

Máire Ní Bhrolcháin is a Senior Lecturer in the Department of Social Statistics at the University of Southampton

Gearóid Ó Tuathaigh is Professor of History at University College Galway

Miriam M. Wiley is a Senior Research Officer at the Economic and Social Research Institute

J.J. Lee is Professor of History at University College Cork

Kieran A. Kennedy is a former Director of the Economic and Social Research Institute

Garret FitzGerald is a former Taoiseach and Minister for Foreign Affairs

Robert W. Hutchinson is Professor of Business Finance at the University of Ulster

Brendan J. Whelan is Director of the Economic and Social Research Institute

Finola Kennedy, an economist, is a contributor to the study, *Family Life and Family Policies in Europe* (Oxford: The Clarendon Press, 1997)

Bláthna Ruane, a member of the Constitution Review Group which reported in May 1996, is a Barrister-at-Law

Charles Lysaght, formerly of the Law Reform Commission, is a Barrister-at-Law

Dermot McAleese is Whately Professor of Political Economy at Trinity College Dublin

Foreword

It was a thoughtful and happy initiative on the part of Dr Kieran Kennedy, former Director of the Economic and Social Research Institute, to organise this series of Thomas Davis lectures in commemoration of the 150th anniversary of the founding of the Statistical and Social Inquiry Society of Ireland. The lectures were broadcast on radio by RTÉ over the winter of 1997/98. They review the main features of social and economic change in Ireland since the Famine. The contributors are all eminent authorities – itself a tribute to the standing and influence of a Society that has been concerned from the outset to analyse, understand and alleviate contemporary problems and displaying always The Spirit of Earnest Inquiry taken by Professor Mary Daly as the title of her succinct history of the Society, published in 1997 by the Institute of Public Administration.

The Statistical and Social Inquiry Society of Ireland has, down the decades, been a valuable meeting ground for academics, farming experts, industrialists, financiers, trade unionists and public servants. For the latter, it has provided a forum not only for professional contributions by official statisticians but also for discreet expression of views on social and economic matters by public servants otherwise enjoined to silence in public on policy issues. Indeed, until *Administration* appeared as the organ of the Institute of Public Administration, it was the only such outlet and, even still, has the advantage of the 'peer review' provided by the sophisticated discussion that follows the delivery of a paper. With many others, I am personally indebted to both these media.

One of my special memories is of the brilliant clarity of Professor George O'Brien's synoptic papers to the Society in the early 1940s on *Economic Relativity* and *Some Recent Developments in Economic Theory*.

The achievement of independence for the Irish Free State in 1922 is a watershed dividing evenly the years of the Society's existence. The lectures in this series naturally give more attention to the years since 1922 and to the profound social and economic changes that have occurred in the new state, but not without advertence to the trends, in some respects disparate, in Northern Ireland. It is safe to say that no-one in that tragic year of 1847 could have predicted such vast changes as have occurred in the size of the population of Ireland and its distribution between country and town or the virtual abandonment of Irish as the common language. Even in 1922 the most optimistic would not have envisaged the improvements in health, education and welfare or in the production of competitive goods and services, which would raise living standards to parity with those of Western Europe. Nor, one must add, would the less positive aspects of today's society have been foreseen – the changes affecting the family and the institution of marriage outlined in Finola Kennedy's lecture, or the coincidence of long-term unemployment, deprivation, drug addiction and criminality dealt with by Charles Lysaght.

The lectures put all this in perspective and provide a perceptive and readable survey of achievements and problems over the Society's broad field of interest. Assembled in this volume, they constitute an invaluable handbook for student and citizen alike.

T.K. Whitaker

1

The Statistical and Social Inquiry Society of Ireland

MARY DALY

The Dublin Statistical Society, the forerunner of the Statistical and Social Inquiry Society was founded in November 1847. Its goal was to promote the study of 'statistical and economical science'. The year 1847 marked the height of the Great Famine, and the Famine was undoubtedly one of the reasons why the Society was established.

Originally the word 'statistics' meant the science of how a state should be organised – a concept that included its laws, provisions for education, public health, welfare, the prevention and punishment of crime, and the economy. During the early nineteenth century, European states began to count the number of people in a country and to keep records of births, marriages and deaths. The word statistics gradually became synonymous with figures.

The first Irish census of population took place in 1821. Three years later, in 1824, a detailed census was carried out in every school in Ireland. In 1847, a few months before the founding of the Dublin Statistical Society, the first agricultural census took place. At that time statistics, in both the modern and the older meaning of the word, appeared to offer objective answers to the major problems facing society, such as the appallingly high death rate in new industrial cities like Manchester, or whether the Irish land system was responsible for the Great Famine.

The first seventy-five years

The founding members of the Dublin Statistical Society were

drawn from the city's professional and intellectual elite: lawyers, academics (including the current and former holders of the Whately chair of economics at Trinity College), a few businessmen, senior officials attached to Dublin Castle, and leading members of the Church of Ireland. They were attracted to the Society by their concern over conditions in Ireland, and by the hope that statistics and economics might offer solutions to the problems that Ireland faced – solutions that avoided the divisiveness of politics or religion. Indeed the constitution of the Dublin Statistical Society specifically prohibited the reading of papers that were likely to produce discussions connected with religious differences or party politics. This clause, which was found in the constitutions of many learned societies in Victorian times, remains in effect to the present day.

The Society, which changed its name in 1862 to the Statistical and Social Inquiry Society of Ireland, provided a meeting place where many of the key figures in Irish political and intellectual life could discuss social and economic questions. Among the favourite topics in the mid-nineteenth century were: whether Ireland was progressing or regressing; was emigration a good or a bad thing; how best to reform the laws relating to bankruptcy; and whether criminal behaviour was a consequence of poverty and illiteracy, or the result of overindulgence in alcohol. The most common topic for discussion was the Irish land question.

For the first twenty-five years of the Society the general mood can be summarised under two headings: optimism and assimilation. The mid-nineteenth century was marked by widespread confidence in the possibility of economic progress, and most members appeared to believe that the Irish economy was progressing in the aftermath of the Famine. Most papers that were read to the Society at this stage suggested that the best recipe for further prosperity was to bring Irish laws and administrative practices into line with those of England and Wales. Such recommendations culminated in two pieces of land legislation passed in 1860: the Deasy and Cardwell Acts. They attempted to transform Irish land law into a mirror image of English land law. W. Neilson Hancock, who was a prominent member of the Society (he presented a total of eighty-eight papers between 1847 and 1883), played a key role in drafting this legislation. By 1870 however, when Gladstone's first Land Act gave legal recognition to the Ulster Custom, and ended the attempt to make Irish land law conform with English law, the Society's influence had waned. The Fenian Rising was largely responsible for the 1870 Land Act, just as the Land League shaped Gladstone's 1881 Land Act.

The growing influence of nationalist politics was not the only factor that weakened the Society's hand. By the late 1870s the belief that economics offered a blueprint for progress was also being questioned throughout Europe, following the onset of a major economic depression. Yet if the Society no longer determined the shape of controversial legislation, such as the land acts, it was extremely influential in other important matters. It retained a long-standing interest in the Poor Law and in the care provided for orphans and for children in need. In this instance drawing comparisons between Irish practices and those in England and Wales proved extremely beneficial. The English Poor Law was much more willing to provide outdoor relief than its Irish counterpart, and this meant that in England widows and their children, and prisoners' wives and families, could remain in their own homes. In Ireland they were generally forced to enter the workhouse. The English Poor Law also attempted to place orphans and abandoned children with foster parents. Many papers read to the Society highlighted these differences, and some members campaigned successfully to persuade the Irish Poor Law to follow the English example. When the National Society for the Prevention of Cruelty to Children was founded in 1889, its first president and many of the founding members were drawn from the Statistical Society.

Women, who were eligible to become associate members, presented several papers on these topics. Indeed the Statistical Society offered possibly the only opportunity in nineteenth-century Ireland for women to address an audience that might include influential politicians and civil servants. The first woman to present a paper was Charlotte Stoker, mother of Bram Stoker, the creator of Count Dracula; in 1863 she spoke about the educational needs of deaf children. Other notable women who addressed the Society before 1900 were Isabella

Tod, a prominent suffragist and Ulster Unionist, who spoke about the cure of habitual drunkards (1875) and the boarding out of pauper children (1878); and Rosa Barrett, a founding member of the National Society for the Prevention of Cruelty to Children. Barrett presented two papers, in 1892 and 1896, concerning the legislative measures introduced in Europe, North America and the British Dominions for the care of neglected children.

The Society investigated other social problems, such as slum housing, urban poverty and tuberculosis. In the aftermath of the Dublin Lock-Out, several sessions in 1914 examined the incomes of Dublin labouring families and the background to the city's housing problem. By then however, the Society had lost much of its earlier momentum. Membership had been declining from the 1880s. Although the Society still attracted leading lawyers, medical doctors and senior civil servants, none of its members were actively involved in the Irish Parliamentary Party or the Sinn Féin and Labour movements. With Home Rule apparently in the offing, the Society seemed to have lost contact with the future leaders of Ireland.

The Irish Free State

In fact the early years of the Irish Free State proved to be one of the most important periods in the Society's history. Many senior officials in the new Irish civil service became active members, and the Society soon established even closer links with the new Irish administration than those it had enjoyed with the Dublin Castle elite. Meetings provided a forum where civil servants, academics, interested members of the public, and the occasional politician, could discuss matters of concern to the new Irish state in a relatively free manner. The fact that the Society's constitution ruled out discussions relating to party politics was probably a blessing in the aftermath of the civil war, though this clause created some difficulties during the 1930s when economic and political opinion was strongly divided over the merits of the Fianna Fáil policies of self-sufficiency and the Economic War. Two papers that had been scheduled for the 1932 session were withdrawn after the general election. While many meetings during these years dealt with technical subjects, such as Irish trade statistics (1924–25, 1937–38), or estimates of Irish national income (Kiernan, 1932–32; Duncan, 1940–41); other papers discussed topics of much wider interest, such as the prospects for Irish agriculture, cinema attendance in the Irish Free State (Beere, 1935–36) and language revivals in Finland, Norway and Wales (Beere, 1929–30).

Many sessions were devoted to the perennial topic of the population of Ireland. This was the theme of the Society's first radio symposium in 1938. The Society set out to refute some of the more fanciful popular opinions concerning population. In 1935 the statistician, Roy Geary, demonstrated that it would be almost impossible for Ireland to regain its pre-famine population of over eight million by the end of the twentieth century. At a meeting of the Society in 1971, Geary recalled that as a result of that paper, he was 'duly savaged for lack of patriotism' by a leading periodical (Knaggs and Keane, 1971). Other members of the Society suggested, during the 1930s, that Ireland's high level of emigration and the prevalence of late marriages could be explained by economic factors, such as the lack of employment opportunities and low living standards (Meenan, 1932–33; Busteed, 1936–37). Such views eventually came to dominate official thinking, through the *Report of the Commission on Emigration and Other Population Problems*, which was published in 1954. A majority of that Commission's members were prominent members of the Society.

During the late 1930s and the 1940s a series of papers produced evidence that had an important bearing on social policies and public health programmes. Statistics showed that mortality from tuberculosis had been rising since 1937 in contrast to the trend in other countries (Counihan and Dillon, 1943–44), and that the incidence of tuberculosis in Dublin was closely associated with poverty and overcrowded housing (Kidney, 1946–47). A study of births in Dublin hospitals during the years 1941 and 1942, carried out by the director of the government statistics service: Stanley Lyon, showed that one-quarter of all children born to fathers in labouring employment were seventh, eighth or higher order births, compared with less than one child in thirteen born to a middle-class family (Lyon,

1942–43 and 1947–48). Others papers by Dr James Deeny (1939–40 and 1943–44), who subsequently became chief medical advisor to the new Department of Health, showed that there was a close association between family poverty and ill health. Another session that examined the subject of regional life tables, showed that a baby boy born in Connacht had a life expectancy ten years greater than a baby boy born in Dublin city (Barry, 1941–42). Research presented by Dr Clancy-Gore, medical officer at Guinness's brewery, in 1943–44 indicated that the standard of nutrition received by a majority of working-class families was either inadequate or barely sufficient to maintain them in good health. These papers strengthened the case for the introduction of children's allowances in 1944. They also suggested that the prevention and treatment of tuberculosis and child health would be priorities for the new Department of Health, which was established in 1947.

The Statistical Society also maintained an active interest in the British government's plans for a welfare state. The sessions devoted to this subject provide some of the most accurate insights into attitudes in Ireland towards the role of the state at this time. When the Society examined the British government's proposals to introduce a comprehensive welfare system in 1943, a prominent Jesuit, Fr Coyne, expressed a fear that 'some very powerful body, say the State, operating through an impersonal bureaucracy' might merely transfer citizens from the 'bondage of poverty and insecurity into the much more de-humanising bondage of regimentation by card-indices, a cold and cruel form of slavery'. His language anticipated the objections that the Catholic Church raised to the Mother and Child Scheme. Coyne was not alone in holding these views. During the same meeting R.J.P. Mortished, a former assistant secretary of the Labour Party and the first chairman of the Labour Court, claimed that the concept of social security carried 'a suggestion of the servile state'.

The period since World War II

In 1945 the Society examined the British government's White Paper, *Employment Policy*. The White Paper recommended that the government should attempt to maintain full employment by increasing investment when the economy was in recession in the manner outlined by the economist, John Maynard Keynes. Although these recommendations were supported by one civil servant, Patrick Lynch, and in a more qualified manner by T.K. Whitaker of the Department of Finance, the majority of speakers concluded that an agricultural economy like Ireland did not need this level of government intervention.

By the late 1950s, however, the stagnant condition of the Irish economy had created a more receptive mood for some form of economic planning. In 1958 the government launched the *Programme for Economic Expansion*, which is generally regarded as paving the way for the prosperity of the 1960s. This programme endorsed most of the recommendations made by the secretary of the Department of Finance, T.K. Whitaker, in another government publication: *Economic Development.* The *Journal of the Statistical and Social Inquiry Society* provides the best opportunity for charting how Whitaker's ideas on Irish economic policy had evolved from the mid-1940s. In 1952, for example, he commented that 'we are living beyond our means, saving too little and consuming too much'. In a lengthy paper read to the Society in 1956, he emphasised the necessity to increase savings and to give priority to productive investment rather than investing in social services, such as housing. Whitaker pointed out that Ireland needed to attract foreign investment and he suggested that 'tariff protection may have to give way to other stimuli, such as grants towards the capital cost of factories or technical training' – a statement that anticipates the future direction of Irish industrial policy.

The 1960s marked a golden age for the Statistical Society. Many views first aired at its meetings had now been accepted as official policy. Economics and statistics appeared to offer a blueprint for a modern and prosperous Ireland, precisely as the Society's founders had hoped in 1847. The economy was growing at an unprecedented rate and economic planning was seen as the key to success. In 1959 the Statistical Society applied to the Ford Foundation for a capital grant to establish an Economic Research Institute. The ERI would provide the detailed economic analysis that was necessary in a modern economy; it would also act as an independent monitor of the government's economic policies. At the same time the Statistical Society organised a series of meetings where the officials responsible for devising and implementing the *Second Programme for Economic Expansion* could discuss their work in a manner that was far removed from the official euphoria. The questions raised at these meetings often exposed the technical limitations of Irish economic planning and raised the possibility that the optimistic goals might not be achieved (Geary, 1963–64; Ryan, 1963–64; Menton, 1964–65).

The Society has consistently offered a corrective to the more extreme views about the Irish economy, whether these were unduly euphoric or too pessimistic. As one member noted, most reports on the Irish economy either paint a picture of unprecedented prosperity or one of unrelenting misery. The reality generally lies somewhere between the clichés of the 'Celtic Tiger' of the 1990s or the bankrupt 'third-world' economy that was said to characterise Ireland during the 1980s.

Throughout its history the Statistical Society has often been one of the first groups, if not indeed the first, to raise crucial questions about the effectiveness of economic and social policy, and it has often highlighted future trends in Irish society. In 1971, at a time when there was widespread rejoicing that the population of Ireland had begun to increase, following over a hundred years in decline, the Society pointed out the drawbacks: Irish taxpayers would have to meet the costs resulting from large numbers of children and old people, and it would prove difficult to create sufficient jobs to employ the growing population (Keane and Knaggs, 1971–72).

In the early 1970s the government believed that the industrial sector would provide the additional jobs that were needed. The Statistical Society had paid very little attention to industrial policy before the late 1960s: this neglect is in itself an important insight into the views of economists and senior public servants on the Irish economy. Since that time, however, industrial policy has become a source of major interest in the Society, and it has also provided some of the liveliest and best-attended sessions. Meetings have examined important questions, such as the relationship between the employment targets set and the number of jobs actually created; the number of jobs lost in existing industry; the benefits to the economy from overseas investment; and the criteria used for subsidising new projects. On several occasions representatives of the Industrial Development Authority discussed industrial policy in considerable detail (McKeon, 1979–80; symposia: 1975–76, 1982–83, 1991–92). Many ideas first aired at these sessions later became incorporated into industrial policy.

Until the 1960s the Society said little about education, probably because the subject threatened to bring it into the prohibited area of religion. With the publication in 1966 of the report, *Investment in Education*, education came to be seen as a key aspect of economic development and consequently an obvious subject for attention. However, the Society was also interested in questions of social equality, with papers examining the socio-economic background of third-level students (Nevin, 1966–67 and 1967–68) and the effectiveness of third-level grants. A symposium in 1981 on the White Paper, *Educational Development*, was highly critical of the fact that government policy failed to address important questions, such as denominational and class segregation within Irish schools.

The population of Ireland has probably been discussed more than any other subject over the Society's 150-year history. On many occasions its meetings have provided advance warning of major changes that were under way. In 1977, when popular attention was focused on the country's high birth-rate, a paper read by a member of the Central Statistics Office noted that Irish marital fertility had begun to decline – something that did not become apparent to the wider public for many years (Keating, 1976–77). In a similar vein, several papers throughout the 1970s and 1980s drew attention to the growing proportion of married women who were in paid employment and examined the factors that had brought about this change (Walsh, 1970–71; Walsh and Whelan, 1973–74; Garvey, 1982–83).

The challenge of increasing specialisation

Few of the statistical societies that were in existence when the Dublin Statistical Society was founded in 1847 survive today. In Britain and the United States, these informal groupings of people, who were drawn together by a common interest in social and economic problems, began to disappear around the end of the nineteenth century; they were replaced by more specialist associations representing professional economists, sociologists, historians and statisticians. The Statistical and Social Inquiry Society probably survived because Ireland was too small to support such bodies. Nevertheless its membership has changed significantly since 1847. The interested amateurs have largely disappeared, though membership remains open to all. Lawyers, a very important and active group until the 1920s, no longer feature in the Society. As a result there have been few papers in recent years on the subject of law reform, though crime and its causes remains a subject of recurring interest. Few medical doctors have addressed the Society since the 1950s and the landmark papers on Irish public health and epidemiology are now presented to more specialist audiences.

The Society established a separate branch in Northern Ireland during the 1950s, at a time when cross-border links were extremely limited. At the beginning there appears to have been a certain reticence about engaging in direct comparisons between economic or social conditions in Northern Ireland and the Irish Republic, presumably because such comparisons might give rise to political controversy. However, in more recent decades an increasing number of papers have adopted a comparative perspective.

For most of its history the Society provided almost the sole opportunity for presenting and discussing research on the Irish economy and Irish social problems. In recent decades, however, with the explosion in the number of graduates, several specialist associations and specialist journals have emerged. At the same time Irish scholars have become more active on the international stage.

All academic disciplines are having to confront the problem of excessive specialisation. A lot of modern economic analysis is presented in such a complex manner that it is no longer intelligible to a wider audience. In 1966, a long-standing member, Professor Joseph Johnston, explained that he rarely attended meetings because 'the Society has gone all econometric and papers are usually incomprehensible to a person of my limited understanding of mathematical matters'

(Attwood, 1966–67). Excessive specialisation poses particular problems for a society that is deliberately multi-disciplinary, but it also presents problems for the wider community. A comprehensive discussion of topics, such as unemployment, social exclusion, or the problems posed by an ageing population, requires the joint efforts of many specialisms; it is also essential that the recommendations and analysis of specialists are intelligible to a wider audience. For the past 150 years the Statistical Society has brought such people together. This role is even more important in the 1990s than in the past.

Conclusion

In 1947, on the occasion of the Society's centenary, its president: Roy Geary noted that 'it is fascinating to observe how in each generation the studies under Society auspices reflected the public interests of the time'. The Society's journal provides a very effective insight into the topics that preoccupied a key section of the Irish elite at different times in the past: housing in 1914, population decline during the 1930s, economic planning during the 1960s, inflation and unemployment in the 1970s. Although it is difficult to prove the extent of the Society's influence, there is little doubt that at times it has played an important role in shaping the policies of both the British administration in Ireland and those of the Irish government. It has also educated sections of Irish society about economic and social issues. Through its journal we can chart the key changes that have taken place in Irish society since the Famine, and the views of a small but influential body of men and women on the condition of Ireland over the past 150 years.

NOTE

This article draws heavily on R.D. Collison Black, *The Statistical and Social Inquiry Society of Ireland, Centenary Volume 1847–1947 with a history of the Society* (Dublin: Eason and Son, 1947); and on Mary E. Daly, *The Spirit of Earnest Inquiry, The Statistical and Social Inquiry Society of Ireland 1847–1997* (Dublin: IPA, 1997). The latter contains a comprehensive index of the Society's Journal, compiled by Helen Litton, in which further details of the papers referred to in the above lecture can be found.

2

The Rise in Living Standards

CORMAC Ó GRÁDA

There are different ways to measure living standards. None are entirely satisfactory, nor do they always tell the same story. Today that rather artificial statistical construct, 'the average Irishman', is three or four inches taller than his counterpart a century and a half ago, and reaches physical maturity a few years earlier. These are two sure indicators that childhood and adolescence are healthier and less stressful now than they were then. Today's 'average Irishman' lives about twice as long as his ancestors of five or six generations ago. Our health and how long we live to enjoy life are clearly important ingredients in the standard of living. The 'average Irishman' may not consume all that many more calories now than he did then – leaving the famine years out of the reckoning, of course – but his calorific needs are less because his lifestyle is more sedentary and his working day shorter. His diet is also much tastier, more balanced and more varied.

Rate of progress

Today our 'average Irishman' earns, after allowing for price inflation, ten or perhaps even twenty times as much as his ancestor of five or six generations ago. Consider briefly a farm labourer or servant on £6 to £10 a year just before the Famine compared with, say, a semi-skilled worker in the 1990s on an annual income of £8,000 to £10,000. The latter's salary could buy six to eight times as many potatoes or ten times as much beef, if he chose to spend his money that way. But his command over other goods and services has risen by much more. Today he could buy, say, twenty times as many shoes, easily twenty times as much cheese, and thirty times as much coal as the farm labourer could in the 1840s. A return journey to New York would have more than exhausted the labourer's annual wage, and would have taken several weeks; today an unskilled worker's wage would buy twenty round-trips, each requiring less than twenty-four hours. The postage stamp, which cost an hour's wages then, can be had for a few minutes' labour now. Similarly with newspapers and popular books.

Comparing the lot of the 'average Irishwoman' then and now would produce even greater betterment. Not only have women's wages risen relative to men's, but so have their literacy rates and their average life span. One hundred and fifty years ago women, on average, died younger than men; now they live about five years longer.

To a considerable extent these changes mirror changes occurring elsewhere (see Fogel, forthcoming), but there is more to the story. Statistical evidence of the poverty of the Irish masses on the eve of the Great Famine is buttressed by a stream of official inquiries and by the accounts of visitors to Ireland who put their impressions to paper. For the bottom one-third or even half of the population, life was harsh and comfortless even by mid-nineteenth century British or West European standards. A German who visited here just before the Famine noted that 'until one has seen the west of Ireland he has no idea that human beings can live in a state of greater misery ... or that a people and cultivated land can look wilder'. What another traveller saw as 'human nature degraded to the lowest state of misery', a third deemed 'shocking for humanity to contemplate'. For the Devon Commissioners, who diagnosed the Irish land system just before the Famine, 'the sufferings borne with exemplary patience' by the Irish poor 'were greater than the people in any other country in Europe had to sustain'. And yet despite all this we should add that, comparatively speaking, the Irish poor were healthy, given their poverty. They were sturdier and they lived longer lives than, say, the Italians or the French at the time (for more on Irish living standards before the Famine see Mokyr, 1985; Ó Gráda, 1994).

Since the Famine, living standards in Ireland have not only risen, they have almost reached the average of an EU-defined Europe. But the pace of change and convergence was very uneven. How uneven? Some measures of the standard of living fit certain periods better than others. In an era when virtually everybody can read and write, literacy rates are of little use; in an age when the number of cars in a country could be numbered in hundreds, vehicle ownership conveys little information. But the big rises in the consumption of tea, sugar, and tobacco in the half-century or so after the Famine – luxury items for the poor in mid-nineteenth century – tell their own stories, as do the improvements in housing conditions and in literacy. The increasing variety of goods bought in village shops, as reflected in surviving ledgers and daybooks, also imply betterment. Let's take the example of a pub grocery in the village of Kilkelly in East Mayo. In 1880 a small range of items, such as sugar, tea, tobacco, flour, Indian meal, and whiskey, dominated its transactions. Less than four decades later the same five items accounted for only one-fifth of transactions, and the shop was supplying customers with quantities of bacon and jam, ready-made clothes and fabrics, and brand name goods such as Jeyes Fluid and Clarendo.

Wage data offer another way of answering the question. The trouble is to obtain information that compares like with like. Some jobs become relatively more skilled or less dangerous over time; others may become more unionised or more exposed to unemployment. Such caveats aside, real wages (i.e. money wages adjusted for changes in the cost of living) rose much more before the early 1920s and again since the 1950s than they did in the interim. Indeed the rise in real wages between the mid-1920s and the mid-1940s was minimal.

National income

Historical estimates of the income or output of the country as a whole offer another useful way of answering questions about changing living standards and convergence. In their favour, they refer to the whole population and make for comparisons not just over time but across countries too. On the other hand, they arguably give too much weight to the incomes of the rich, and thus ideally need to be complemented by information about the distribution of income. Comparing national income over time and with other economies can tell us a few interesting stories.

Our best-guess estimates of Irish national income in the wake of the Famine and on the eve of World War I imply considerable convergence on neighbouring countries in the interim. Between 1845 and 1914 Ireland gained in the standard-of-living stakes not only on Britain, but also on countries such as Belgium, Norway and Spain. Population had a lot to do with this. On the eve of the Famine, it is worth remembering that Ireland contained more people than the whole of Scandinavia, that is Denmark, Sweden, Finland and Norway, put together. Yet by 1914, Scandinavia would outpeople Ireland by a ratio of three to one. The same applies for Belgium and Holland combined. Portugal and Scotland, with far fewer people than Ireland in 1845, would contain more in 1914. The population of England and Wales, less than double that of Ireland in 1845, was eight times as high by 1914. Ireland's dramatic demographic adjustment was largely responsible for the convergence in living standards.

The same best-guess estimate of national income on the eve of World War I underpins Professor Joseph Lee's critique of Irish economic performance since independence. In *Ireland 1912–1985: Politics and Society* (1989), Lee argued that Ireland had slid down the European income league table after 1922. Lee's work, published in the wake of several years of fiscal retrenchment and falling living standards, was the best-known of several studies arguing that 'independent Ireland' had failed, for whatever reason, to deliver the goods. The outcome becomes plausible once one remembers that Lee's six decades include the 1920s and 1930s, when there was very little growth; the Emergency years, when the economy contracted; and the 1950s, another dismal decade of near-zero growth.

Still, the rise in living standards since the 1960s has been impressive enough. The extraordinary performance over the last decade or so has been enough to compensate, and perhaps more than compensate, for the 'also ran' status of an earlier era. National accounts imply catch-up both vis-à-vis the UK and the rest of the EU. The message conveyed by the national accounts is confirmed by other indicators, such as spending on consumer durables and foreign holidays, and by lower infant mortality rates. Moreover, unemployment insurance, public and private pension schemes, and medical care have greatly reduced the privation attendant on job loss and illness.

National income data also provide an answer, though a necessarily crude one, to a question that often crops up: how did life for the Irish poor a century and a half ago compare to that of the poor of, say, Somalia or Ethiopia today? Linking historical Irish and contemporary Somalian and Ethiopian national income estimates to British estimates offers a round-about answer. This indicates that the Irish on the eve of the Famine were better off than the people of Ethiopia in the recent past, and about on a par with the people of Somalia. But by the same reckoning, living standards in Great Britain then, were roughly on a par with those of Indonesia or Egypt today.

One further curious implication of recent national accounts data is that the traditionally backward economy of the Irish Republic has now overtaken that of Northern Ireland, in terms of output per head and output per worker, If sustained, this achievement marks quite a remarkable historic reversal. This chapter, however, is examining living standards, and exchequer transfers from London mean that living standards remain higher in Northern Ireland than in the Republic. Indeed, reckoned in terms of consumer durables, such as cars, micro-waves, central heating, video recorders and telephones, the gap in living standards between Northern Ireland and the rest of the UK is now small. But thc South has been gaining not only on Northern Ireland: the latest OECD data suggest that Ireland's private consumption per head rose from 57 to 84 per cent of British levels between 1987 and 1995.

Though the correlation across countries between national income, on the one hand, and other proxies for living standards, such as literacy and health and longevity, on the other, is good, it is far from perfect. Some countries, very poor in terms of gross domestic product per head, perform much better in terms of literacy or life span. The human development index (HDI), devised by the United Nations, is an admittedly crude indicator of living standards that seeks to take account of these considerations. It combines measures of longevity, level of education and income. The measures of life span and schooling tend to be more equally distributed than income; this measure implicitly gives heavier weighting to the welfare of the poor. HDI data, reported in a recent study by Professor Nick Crafts of the London School of Economics, suggest that gross domestic product may underestimate human development in Ireland in both 1913 and 1950.

The distribution of income

The national accounts can tell us about averages, but distribution matters too. In Ireland it seems self-evident that the rich are, and always have been, better educated and healthier than the poor. In the past health differences were reflected in height differences: in the mid-nineteenth century the illiterate poor were, on average, about half an inch to an inch smaller than the not-so-poor who could read and write. Differences in longevity by socio-economic background in the same period are unavailable, but they were almost certainly greater than they are today.

A recent account describes Ireland before 1914 as extremely unequal, in ways that we cannot, perhaps, nowadays easily imagine. Though this claim is not backed up by any data, there is no denying that the gap between rich and poor was greater then than now. Labour was cheap then and capital expensive; that is why professional people could afford menservants, maids and gardeners in a manner impossible for even the very rich now. Daniel O'Connell's earnings as a leading barrister, £6,000 to £7,000 a year, would have been enough to hire sixty or seventy servants; though today's barristers enjoy comforts O'Connell would not have even dreamed of, they probably would be unable to emulate him in that respect. Unlike O'Connell, they pay income tax. The gap between professional incomes and the wages for semi-skilled work is still great, but certainly not as great as in O'Connell's time.

Poverty and inequality have spatial, historical and interpersonal dimensions. In Ireland trends in the regional or spatial aspect, long highlighted, are perhaps the easiest to capture. The Great Famine of the 1840s killed one person in four in parts of the west, while parts of the east and north escaped relatively unscathed. The contrast highlights an east-west regional problem, which persisted long into the period reviewed here. While the Famine reduced regional inequality in brutal fashion it by no means eliminated it, and in subsequent decades repeated attempts were made to attenuate regional disadvantage. The rhetoric of public representatives and community organisations in the west continues to be one of under-privilege.

Yet if Ireland's regional problem is defined in terms of the gap in standards between those living in advantaged and disadvantaged counties, then it has been virtually eliminated during the decades reviewed here. Transfers and subsidies both from Dublin and from the EU played a part in this – by increasing purchasing power, improving infrastructure and providing better health care and transport – but emigration from the poorer counties has been mainly responsible for closing the gap. At the outset, the higher emigration from the west was due to relative poverty. That emigration in turn reduced the income gap between counties. In 1936 the poorest of the four provinces, Connacht, contained 17.7 per cent of the South's population, but in 1971 its share was down to only 13 per cent. Since the 1970s the west has almost managed to maintain its share of the population, and in 1991 Connacht's share was still 12 per cent. Emigration rates across counties have also converged in striking fashion.

The strong negative association across counties, between the rate of population change and the rise in the number of consumer durables per head, supports the role played by emigration in the convergence in living standards. Where population fell most is, by and large, where housing conditions improved most. Unemployment and emigration, two other correlates of poverty, are also much more evenly spread across the country now than they were two or five decades ago. In Ireland today poverty and deprivation are not only more visible, but also probably more intense, in Dublin and Cork working-class suburbs than in the rural west.

As the regional convergence in living standards has come about mainly through emigration, it has affected the viability of many parish and village communities in the west. Emigration (and partition) has left the Irish Republic with a rather lopsided population distribution, with Dublin city and its hinterland accounting for nearly one-third of the total. But could it have been otherwise without further sacrifices in average living standards? In agriculture it seems fair to say that there was little that policy could achieve in the west, in the face of an average farm size too small to allow the requisite productivity change. Nor have decades of public spending through agencies such as Údarás na Gaeltachta and the Industrial Development Authority, and the continued subsidisation of communications, produced much of enduring value on the manufacturing front. Of course, there are exceptions: Galway city has done particularly well. But probably more effective in redressing the regional imbalance would have been a commitment from the outset to locate more government services and more educational institutions outside Dublin.

The limited data available on regional incomes suggest significant convergence. Other information confirms this outcome. For instance, as late as 1961, nearly 75 per cent of houses in Leitrim lacked any sanitary facilities, as did over 60 per cent of houses in Clare, Kerry, Longford and Roscommon. Three decades later, Roscommon was worst placed, but its 20 per cent marked both a big improvement and relative catch-up. Official data on radio and television licences and on car ownership also register both improvement and regional convergence. In 1951 Ireland had 110 radio licences per thousand population. In 1991 radios no longer required licences, but there were over twice as many television licences per thousand population as there had been radio licences in 1951.

The evolution of private car ownership serves as another handy informal index of living standards across countries. It can also provide a rough ranking of the trend in living standards across Irish counties. In Ireland, the number of cars per thousand population rose from 14 in 1936 to over 100 in the mid-1960s, and over 300 in 1997. Differences across counties in the ratio of cars to people have plummeted since the 1930s.

Nor is there much similarity between the pattern thirty or forty years ago and now. If one compares new registrations of bigger cars, the levelling effect across counties has been more marked (for more on this see Ó Gráda, 1997).

In Northern Ireland too, the regional gap in living standards has narrowed over the last half-century. Administrative boundary changes in 1971 rule out continuous comparisons, but the data on housing amenities in 1971 and 1991 tell an important part of the story. In Fermanagh in 1971 half of all households still depended on outside toilet facilities, as did nearly 40 per cent in Strabane, compared to about 5 per cent in North Down. By 1991 nearly all had indoor toilets. The gap between the best and worst-off districts was still considerable in 1971, but had almost vanished two decades later. In Northern Ireland too, emigration and transfers were mainly responsible for the reduction in regional inequality.

Public policy

Public policy can influence the distribution of wealth and income and help to reduce poverty. In this sense the policies of the pre-1932 Cosgrave administrations are likely to have increased the gap between rich and poor. It is true that they were fiscally constrained by the needs to repair civil war damage and to establish an economic reputation, but there was a hard edge too to the pronouncements of government spokesmen. Social Welfare Minister, P.J. Burke, supported the cut in the old age pension in 1924 with the claim that 'one of the most serious defects of the Irish character is this tendency to dependence of one kind or another'. 'The number of people who lead a parasitic existence', he continued, including the unfortunate old age pensioners, '[was] increasing relative to the number of people who are striving to make an honest living'. But that was mild stuff compared with Patrick McGilligan's announcement in the Dáil a few months later, in the course of a debate on unemployment, that 'people may have to die in this country and die of starvation'. Cumann na nGaedheal abolished assistance to the uninsured unemployed – the dole – at the end of 1924.

The first detailed estimate of income distribution in Ireland refers to the 1938–44 period. The data on personal incomes are incomplete, but they are still useful. Though the revelation that the top 3,000 or so took 5 per cent of all income in 1943 must have made UCD economist George O'Brien's assertion, that 'the distribution of income in Éire is not marked by any high degree of inequality', hard to swallow, O'Brien was probably not far from the truth in comparative terms.

Insofar as economic and social policy was concerned, the young Fianna Fáil was far more indulgent and populist in its attitude to welfare than its predecessor. Nor was this merely a matter of rhetoric: soon after gaining power, de Valera's party extended the dole to small farmers and increased the old age pension and disability benefits. In 1944, it introduced a system of family allowances to families with three children or more. The inter-party administration that succeeded Fianna Fáil in 1948 was also more welfare-oriented than pre-1932 Cumann na nGaedheal. Systematic ideological differences between subsequent administrations in this sphere are difficult to detect. Fianna Fáil's introduction of free second-level education in 1966 was matched by big increases in social welfare spending after 1973, under the late Labour leader Brendan Corish.

Yet in recent comparisons of income distribution in European countries, Ireland emerges in not such a favourable light; in one study of income distribution in the 1980s, Ireland came last out of fourteen. In mitigation, it might be argued that Ireland's income distribution was not unduly unequal, given its stage of economic development. Suppose that relative poverty rates were a good deal higher in Ireland than in more developed EU countries, but not unlike those found in Greece, Portugal and, to a lesser extent, Spain. Besides being out of date, that defence ignores the fact that in the 1980s all these countries had only recently emerged from fascism. Besides, its rather disheartening implication that reformist politics cannot reduce income or wealth inequality, since they are tightly constrained by a country's degree of development, is not corroborated by other studies. And even if they were, that excuse is no longer there for the 'greyhound economy' of the late 1990s.

Finally, a caveat. I have focused on what people had and have, rather than how they felt or feel about it. Insofar as people's command over material goods influences how happy they are, the strategy is justifiable. But measuring happiness directly is a much trickier business. For what they are worth, national and international surveys of happiness indicate that it has not grown in tandem with income. Had Gallup or MORI been around in, say, the 1850s and 1860s and asked a sample of Irish people to describe themselves on some happiness scale, they might well have declared themselves to be, on average, as happy as a sample similarly chosen today. In the words of the song, 'you don't know what you've got till it's gone'; happiness is more about what we are used to, and what we see others having, than simply what we ourselves have.

FURTHER READING

Crafts, N.F.R. (1997), 'The Human Development Index and Changes in Standards of Living: Some Historical Comparisons', *European Review of Social History*, 1, 299–*322*

Fogel, R. W. (forthcoming), *The Escape from Hunger and Premature Death 1700–2100, The 1996 Ellen McArthur Lectures*, Cambridge: Cambridge University Press

Lee, J.J. (1989), *Ireland 1912–1985: Politics and Society*, Cambridge: Cambridge University Press

Mokyr, J. (1985), *Why Ireland Starved: A Quantitative and Analytical History of the Irish Economy 1800–1850*, (2nd ed.), London: Allen and Unwin

Ó Gráda, C. (1994), *Ireland: A New Economic History 1780–1939*, Oxford: Oxford University Press

Ó Gráda, C. (1997), *A Rocky Road: The Irish Economy since the 1920s*, Manchester: Manchester University Press

3

Is Ireland Underpopulated?

MÁIRE NÍ BHROLCHÁIN

If the Republic of Ireland[1] were as densely populated as the Netherlands is today, we would number 26 million people. That would make Ireland the nation with the fifth largest population in the European Union. If the 26 million were distributed in the same way as Ireland's population is now, Dublin would be the same size as London, and Cork would be a metropolis of over one million people.

Is this social science fiction? Could we indeed have become a nation of 26 million people? To reach this figure from our 1841 population of 6.5 million, the population of Ireland would have had to grow at an average of just under 1 per cent per annum. Average growth rates of this order were, in fact, reached by several other European countries between 1841 and the present day.[2] So, an Irish population of 26 million today would have been within the bounds of recent historical experience in Europe. The Netherlands is the most heavily populated country in Europe, and so might not be an ideal demographic role model. As an alternative, we could consider Germany's density level, which would equip Ireland with a population of 16 million; or that of France, which would make us 8 million strong. In principle, and from a purely demographic standpoint, either of these two figures could easily have been reached from our 1841 population.

As it is, in 1996 we numbered 3.6 million people (26 counties), just over half the 6.5 million enumerated in the 1841 census (8.2 million in the 32 counties) and we are now (with 51 persons per square kilometre) one of the most sparsely populated countries in Europe. From its highest point in 1845, Ireland's population went into a long decline that came to a halt only in 1961. In marked contrast, other European nations experienced substantial population growth over this period. In 1841 the population of the 26 counties was one and a half times that of Belgium, but the Belgians are now three times as numerous as we are. Ireland's population at that time was twice that of Sweden and of the Netherlands but the Swedes now outnumber us by two and a half to one and the Dutch by four to one.[3] All European countries, large and small, saw their populations grow from the middle of the nineteenth century; all except Ireland. Our population experience is, therefore, unique in modern times.[4]

How and why is this? In what follows, I will be looking at *how*, in an accounting sense, Ireland's population declined up to 1961. I will also consider *why* it happened. The 'how' of Ireland's population decline can be answered fairly readily, thanks to the research and scholarship of Ireland's economic and social historians. But the question 'why' is more difficult and potentially more controversial.

The arithmetic of population change is very simple: births minus deaths plus or minus net emigration equals population change. A positive balance will result in growth and a negative one will bring decline. Along with fertility, mortality and migration, marriage is relevant too, since the frequency of marriage can boost or restrain the number of births. So, four key ingredients – marriage rates, birth rates, death rates and emigration – have gone into the making of the story of Ireland's population over the last 150 years. I will focus especially on the second half of the nineteenth century, since it was then that the bulk of our population loss occurred, and that our unique population history was forged.[5]

Was marriage the culprit?

We begin with marriage and a major discovery about historical marriage patterns. Imagine the map of Europe with a line drawn from Trieste, on the eastern side of the Gulf of Venice, to St Petersburg, on the Gulf of Finland. This imaginary line, discovered by John Hajnal the Anglo-Hungarian demographer, marks a major division in European marriage customs. In European countries to the south and east of the line, marriage was by tradition early and very few remained unmarried. To the north and west of the line, marriage was traditionally at a fairly late age and sizeable proportions – about one in ten – of men and women remained single (Hajnal, 1965). Ireland's marriage habits around 1841 conformed exactly to her geo-political position in North West Europe: marriage was late and about one in ten never married.[6]

On the eve of the Famine, there was nothing remarkable about marriage in Ireland. However, in its wake the frequency of marriage declined steadily and by the turn of the century the proportion staying single had more than doubled. Around 1911 as many as one-quarter of Irish people (27 per cent of men; 25 per cent of women) remained unmarried (Fitzpatrick, 1985, Table 1; Walsh, 1970). Indeed Ireland acquired for itself a reputation among social scientists as being almost averse to marriage, and some have even wondered out loud whether there was something the matter with the national sex drive. In fact, reports that the 'passion between the sexes' was less ardent in turn of the century Ireland than elsewhere are greatly exaggerated. Though the proportions never marrying in Ireland in the latter half of the nineteenth century were well above the European average, similar proportions were recorded in several other countries and regions (Guinnane, 1997, p. 97).[7] Nevertheless, the numbers remaining unmarried reached unprecedented proportions in the mid-1930s, particularly among men: 39 per cent of 40–44 year old men and 27 per cent of women of this age had never married (Ó Gráda, 1997, p. 196). And while the proportion remaining single declined over time, it was still relatively high as recently as 1971. Still, exceptionally low proportions marrying were a feature of the not too distant past, rather than of the 'traditional' Ireland of the nineteenth century.

Was there a scarcity of births in Ireland?

Was this decline in marriage frequency responsible for Ireland's protracted population loss? Were there too few births because of the low frequency of marriage? The answer to this question is, on the whole, 'no'. The reason why low marriage rates did not curb the birth rate is because at that time those people who did marry had large families. Fertility within marriage in the Ireland of those years was high by European standards. Evaluated against the world-record fertility levels reached by a small Anabaptist sect, known as the Hutterites, married couples in nineteenth-century Ireland were just 16 per cent short of what we might describe as the Hutterite 'baby standard'. So, prolific childbearing within Irish marriages offset the high proportion remaining single, with the net result that, overall, birth rates were about the same in Ireland as elsewhere in West Europe in the second half of the nineteenth century.

Mortality

We have found then that neither marriage rates nor birth rates were, in an accounting sense, the root cause of population decline in Ireland. Nor, indeed, were death rates. Except during years of crisis, mortality in nineteenth-century Ireland was at the same level as in other West European countries at the time. There is some suggestion that death rates in pre-famine Ireland were lower than the European average. A contributory factor may have been that the staple diet of the poor: potatoes and milk, though no doubt tedious, was a nutritious one. Objective evidence of an indirect kind backs up this assessment. Though poor before the Famine, Irish people seem to have been among the tallest people in Europe, and since average height can be considered an indirect indicator of general health in a population, this suggests an Irish advantage in health, due almost certainly to diet and perhaps also the low level of urbanisation (Ó Gráda, 1993, Chapter 1; Ó Gráda, 1994, Appendix 4.1).

The mortality resulting from the Famine was, of course, exceptional. Over and above the deaths that would have occurred in ordinary circumstances, an estimated one million people died as a result of the Famine (Boyle and Ó Gráda, 1986). Heavy though that toll was, population numbers could have recovered if it were not for the other destructive legacy of the Famine: mass emigration.

Emigration

Our search for the causes of Ireland's population decline brings us finally to the question of emigration. And emigration is, indeed, the origin of the 120-year decline in Ireland's population up to 1961. The Famine propelled a spectacular exodus from Ireland in the second half of the nineteenth century. Though sizeable before the Famine, emigration took on truly massive proportions in its wake. In just ten years, from 1846 to 1855, two and a half million people emigrated from Ireland, over a quarter of the entire population.[8] That number is equal to the entire present population of the 26 counties excluding Dublin. Although the decades that followed saw a progressive decline in emigration rates, departures were still very high. Between 1855 and 1914, four million people emigrated from Ireland. Altogether eight million people emigrated from Ireland between 1801 and 1921: a truly massive exodus (Fitzpatrick, 1984).

The demographic balance sheet is, then, as follows. For a century and a half, births in Ireland have outnumbered deaths, except during crisis years. This positive rate of natural increase should have resulted, as it did elsewhere in Europe, in steady population growth. However, until recently, not only did the high level of emigration cancel the excess of births over deaths, it resulted in a prolonged decline in numbers. Mass emigration over a long period, beginning especially during the Famine, is the answer to the question of how Ireland's population loss occurred. Hard on the heels of the question of how it happened is the question: why?

Why did Ireland's population decline?

Since emigration has been the root cause of Ireland's population loss, the question why Ireland's population declined in the century or so to 1961 is now transformed into another: why was emigration from Ireland so heavy and so prolonged? In considering this difficult question, we should remember that nineteenth-century Ireland was not alone in sending large numbers of emigrants overseas. The nineteenth century was a time of spectacular migration from almost all parts of Europe. Between 1815 and 1930, 52 million people emigrated from

Europe (Baines, 1995). In that great throng the Irish were just one national group among many, and not the most numerous. Britain, in fact, was the origin of the largest overseas migrant stream of over 11 million emigrants. Second was Italy, the origin of a further 10 million emigrants. Ireland was the third largest, with 7 million emigrants (Baines, 1995, Table 2). The most common destination was the United States, which became home to a vast and diverse array of migrant Europeans: apart from the British, the Italians and the Irish, millions of Germans, Swedes, Norwegians, Poles, Czechs, Austrians, Hungarians, Russians and Ukrainians, among others, left Europe to seek their fortunes in the New World (Bogue, 1959).

How is it then, that in spite of large-scale emigration the populations of other European countries grew while Ireland's was falling? The answer is, of course, that emigration from Ireland was much larger in relative terms than from other European countries. From 1850 to 1899 Ireland lost through emigration between 10 per cent and 20 per cent of her population each decade.[9] In no other European country was the toll so high for so long.[10] The lower emigration rates elsewhere in Europe allowed moderate to high levels of population growth.

Let us pause briefly to take stock. In looking for the reason for Ireland's protracted loss in population to 1961, we have found that the main culprit was prolonged emigration on a large scale from the middle of the nineteenth century. But since emigration from Ireland in the nineteenth century was part of a more general European phenomenon, we reformulate our original question and replace it with three subsidiary questions. Why was there such a mass migration from Europe in the second half of the nineteenth century? Were the origins of Irish emigration the same as in the rest of Western Europe? And finally, why the much heavier rate of emigration from Ireland?

The full story of the mass migration from Europe during the nineteenth century is not yet known but it seems likely that both 'push' and 'pull' factors were at work. That is, emigration was prompted both by unfavourable circumstances in the home country and by the lure of better prospects in the destination country. In the nineteenth century, Ireland and her West European neighbours experienced high population growth rates and these resulted in an expansion in numbers that their economies were simply unable to absorb. High rates of natural increase combined with the growing pains of industrialisation, and especially the decline in cottage industry, gave rise to widespread poverty. Labour shortages and higher wage rates in the New World – North America, South America and Australia – provided a strong impetus to overseas migration. A further stimulus to emigration is what might be called the 'gravitational attraction' exerted by the number of emigrants from the home country who were already settled abroad. So, poverty and underdevelopment together with rapid population growth were the forces driving the mass migration from Europe in the nineteenth century (Hatton and Williamson, 1994).

Ireland's emigrants were influenced by the same 'push' and 'pull' factors as emigrants from other European nations. But there was an additional and decisive element in the Irish experience: the Famine. The Famine resulted directly, as we have seen, in the huge exodus of two and a half million people between 1846 and 1855. On top of that, it was almost certainly the indirect cause of the persistence of high emigration rates through the 'gravitational attraction' exercised by the large stock of emigrants already settled abroad. Past emigration generated further emigration and the flow became self-sustaining.[11]

Towards an explanation of Irish population trends

The Famine was, therefore, a pivotal event in Irish population history. It emerges as the key to the scale of nineteenth-century emigration from Ireland. It is therefore the origin of the peculiarity of Ireland's population history when contrasted with that of our European neighbours. But what accounts for the Famine? This is, of course, one of the largest questions in Irish history, and one which is still emotive, even 150 years on.

There are at least two distinct views on the origins of the Famine, which we can summarise roughly as 'Ireland was asking for it' versus 'Ireland was unlucky'. The first of these was, until recently, the consensus among historians – though the consensus appears to have been based more on its plausibility and intellectual convenience than on an appraisal of solid historical fact. The view that Ireland invited catastrophe is based on the ideas of the English parson and economist, Thomas Malthus. Malthus believed that one of the ways in which population numbers were kept in check was that excessive population growth would put increasing pressure on resources, thus reducing living standards, creating widespread poverty and ultimately resulting in wars, epidemics of disease or famine. The ensuing rise in death rates would remove the surplus population, thereby bringing numbers back into balance with available resources. So the argument goes: the Famine was a catastrophe waiting to happen because Ireland's population growth had been too rapid in the preceding decades. Malthus himself, who died in 1834, appears not to have viewed Ireland as being of much relevance to his theory about population and resources, a telling historical detail (Ó Gráda, 1989, pp. 26–7; Ó Gráda, 1993, Chapter 1).

The 'Ireland was asking for it' school of thought has been vigorously challenged by recent research, which finds that it does not fit the historical facts (Mokyr, 1983; Ó Gráda, 1993). From the middle of the eighteenth century, Ireland's population went into a phase of sustained growth, but so also did that of almost every other European nation (Livi-Bacci, 1997, pp. 74–79). Rates of growth varied from place to place, and the rate in Ireland was on the high side. Nonetheless, at the beginning of the nineteenth century several other European countries were experiencing population growth rates of the same order as Ireland.[12] Furthermore, the pace of Irish population growth was falling in the immediate pre-famine period, due to delayed marriage and sizeable emigration. A subsistence crisis was not 'inevitable', since self-regulation of population numbers was already under way through a less calamitous adjustment process (Ó Gráda, 1993). Finally, the results of a detailed econometric analysis of the evidence are inconsistent with the proposition that pre-famine Ireland was overpopulated (Mokyr, 1983, Chapter 3). There are, then, good reasons for doubting that the Famine was a disaster waiting in the wings.

An alternative reading is that the Famine was a tragic historical accident, the scale of which could not have been foreseen. Famines were a recurring feature of the European demographic régime up to the early nineteenth century. One estimate puts the frequency of subsistence crises in Europe during the sixteenth, seventeenth and eighteenth centuries at two, three, four or even more per century (Livi-Bacci, 1997, p. 85). But harvest failure on the scale of the Great Irish Famine was altogether unknown (Ó Gráda, 1993, Chapter 3). Even so, once it had happened it seems clear in retrospect that much of the excess mortality due to the Famine could have been avoided by administrative measures (Mokyr, 1983, Chapter 10). That such steps were not taken is a reflection of the ideology of non-intervention of the British government of the day: as one contemporary observer put it, 'Ireland died of political economy' (John Mitchel, quoted in Ó Gráda, 1995). It also indicates that the dreadful toll of the Famine was almost certainly due as much to Ireland's historical, economic and political situation vis-à-vis Britain, as to repeated harvest failure. This was, in other words, a subsistence crisis with a decidedly political dimension.[13]

Consequences

Ironically, the role of the Famine in Irish history may well be exactly the opposite of how it is conventionally portrayed. Instead of providing a textbook example of the hazards of overpopulation, the depopulation caused by the Famine may instead be a prime example of the economic disadvantages of underpopulation. Ireland is now one of Europe's least densely populated countries, and has until very recently been one of the least prosperous. Is there a link between the two? Is Ireland's population small because economic growth has been slow? Or is it the other way round: has the small size of our population inhibited economic growth?

Danish economist, Ester Boserup, has proposed a theory that stands the Malthusian approach on its head in precisely this way (Boserup, 1965; 1981; 1990). In her view, population pressure can be a positive force by creating the conditions for technological change and economic development. Not only is there economic strength in numbers, population growth generates an economic dynamism of its own. It is easy to see the more obvious economic benefits that a larger population could bring, especially to a small economy, such as greater specialisation resulting in efficiency gains; greater complexity of social organisation; economies of scale in relation to infrastructure, for example transport, communications, education and health systems; larger home markets for indigenous enterprise; and a more attractive environment for inward investment (Livi-Bacci, 1997, Chapter 3).

The true significance of population in recent Irish history may be that post-famine Ireland has lacked and continues to lack population pressure and its associated economic benefits. On this interpretation, the Famine played a major role in removing growing population pressure and thus eliminated a crucial potential spur to economic development. As one historian has put it: 'the overall result of heavy and prolonged emigration was to mitigate the need for economic transformation ... and to reduce ... Ireland's attractiveness as a field for investment' (Fitzpatrick, 1984, p. 38). The Famine also ensured that mass emigration would continue to have this effect by establishing a propensity to emigrate that became self-sustaining in the long term. Emigration was etched into the national subconscious as an acceptable and even attractive way to make a livelihood.

In Ester Boserup's perspective, population has a more central role in influencing economic performance than economic orthodoxy would ordinarily allow. Where economists would portray population as driven by economic forces, Boserup's theory turns this around, making population one of the motors of economic development. Economists and demographers have in recent years been attempting to combine these two perspectives, in searching for a more comprehensive account of the relationship between population and resources (Lee, 1986; Bonneuil, 1994). Maybe such a synthesis will, in time, give us a better understanding of the Irish case.

Recent experience

Before closing, let us take a brief look at contemporary Ireland. Having diverged for over a century from the demographic experience of her neighbours, Ireland's demographic profile has been converging with the rest of Europe in the last couple of decades. For much of the last fifty years Ireland was well ahead of other North West European countries in the reproduction stakes, but fertility is now below replacement level. Indeed, fertility is currently higher in Sweden and Iceland than in Ireland. Having risen in the decades after the Second World War, marriage rates have been declining very recently, but this is partly compensated for by an increase in cohabitation (Walsh, 1985). Separation and divorce are on the increase and the proportion of births that occur outside marriage has been rising steeply (Kennedy, 1989). These trends are common not only to much of Europe but to the developed world in general.

Some effects of our recent demographic history are still to be seen in Ireland's population structure. It is only very recently that Ireland joined the rest of Europe in arriving at fertility rates below the crucial replacement level of 2.1 births per woman. One of the after-effects of that recent high fertility is that Irish children have many more siblings than do other European children. In 1991, two-thirds of Irish children lived in a family of three or more children but this is true of only one-third of children elsewhere in the European Union (Eurostat, 1996). Another consequence of the recency of relatively high birth rates in Ireland is that Ireland has the youngest population in the European Union, with four in ten people aged under twenty-five; the EU-average is one-third. This means that relatively large age cohorts will be working their way through the population age structure in the coming decades. As a result, Ireland's population has, currently, a built-in potential for further growth, even if fertility remains at its present level and provided of course that emigration remains low.

Life expectancy is just a little below that of other West European nations, probably due to the gap in prosperity between Ireland and the rest of Europe in past decades. We are, however, well ahead of East Europe in this respect and, in fact, male life expectancy is currently higher in Ireland than in the United States. Ireland's population has been growing slowly since 1961 and there is still an excess of births over deaths. But the gap between these two is narrowing and emigration can still very easily tip the balance and result in overall population loss. Whether it does so depends on the performance of the economy, and the recent economic expansion in Ireland bodes well in that respect. The importance of an expansion in employment opportunities to avoid population decline has long been recognised (Kennedy, 1975). It is greatly to be hoped that a virtuous circle is in the course of being established in which economic growth promotes demographic growth and vice versa. Now, as always, population and economy in Ireland are closely bound up together.

ACKNOWLEDGEMENTS

I am indebted to Cormac Ó Gráda and to David Coleman for their generous help in preparing this paper.

NOTES

1 Except where qualified, the term 'Ireland' is used here to refer to the 26 counties

2 These are: Belgium, Denmark and the Netherlands. The calculations are based on Table A5 of Mitchell (1992) and Eurostat (1996)

3 Figures based on Table A5 of Mitchell (1992) and Eurostat (1996)

4 Though Ireland's population experience is unique in modern Europe, over the long course of history many human populations and their civilisations have experienced cycles of growth and decay: see, for example, Cohen (1995, Figure 3.1) for a depiction of population swings in Egypt between 750 BC and the present day

5 Of the 3.66 million decline in population that occurred between 1841 and 1971, 70 per cent had occurred in the three decades from 1841 to 1871 and almost all (94 per cent) by the turn of the century

6 In 1841, the average age at marriage of men was 29.9 and of women 26.5. The proportion of men remaining single was 10.8 per cent and of women 12.5 per cent (Fitzpatrick, 1985, Tables 1 and 2). These latter figures relate in fact to men and women aged 45 to 54, in order to approximate the proportions never married by age 50. This is the conventional limiting age by which proportions ever/never married are assessed in demography, both because the vast majority of marriages occur by this age and because marriage at age 50+ will have negligible implications for fertility

7 Guinnane (1997) comments that while 20 per cent of Irish men aged 45 to 49 in 1900 had never married, the proportion in Iceland was 19 per cent and in Belgium 16 per cent. Among Irish women of this age, 17 per cent had never married and this was the same as in Belgium and Switzerland, while the proportions were higher in Iceland, Portugal and Sweden

8 The average annual number who emigrated between 1846 and 1855 was five times the yearly average during the three decades preceding the Famine (Mokyr and Ó Gráda, 1982)

9 Annual average emigration rates were between 9.7 and 19.0 per 1000 in this period (Hatton and Williamson, 1994, Table 1)

10 Italy comes nearest, reaching (gross) emigration rates of 8.65 per 1000 in 1890–99 and 17.97 per 1000 in 1900–13

11 An estimate of the size of this 'magnetic' attraction is that for every 1000 previous emigrants abroad a further 20 were 'pulled' to emigrate every year. On this reckoning, 2.5 million emigrants abroad would through this mechanism alone attract 50,000 further emigrants every year (Hatton and Williamson, 1994)

12 Growth rates of 1.5 per cent were reached in England, Scotland, Scandinavia, the Netherlands and Germany as well as in Ireland in the early decades of the nineteenth century (Flinn, 1981, Chapter 6)

13 The political aspects of the Famine could be clarified by comparative research on other subsistence crises, especially in Europe, before and since. Comparisons of nineteenth-century Europe with the contemporary Third World are well wide of the mark (Ó Gráda, 1995)

REFERENCES

Baines, D. (1995), *Emigration from Europe 1815–1930*, Cambridge: Cambridge University Press

Bogue, D. (1959), *The Population of the United States*, Illinois: The Free Press of Glencoe

Bonneuil, N. (1994), 'Malthus, Boserup and population viability', *Mathematical Population Studies*, 5(1), pp. 107–119

Boserup, E. (1965), *The Conditions of Agricultural Growth*, London: George Allen and Unwin

Boserup, E. (1981), *Population and Technological Change*, Chicago: University of Chicago Press and Oxford: Blackwell

Boserup, E. (1990), *Economic and Demographic Relationships in Development*, London: Johns Hopkins University Press

Boyle, P. and Ó Gráda, C. (1986), 'Fertility trends, excess mortality, and the Great Irish Famine', *Demography*, 23 (4), pp. 543–562

Cohen, J.E. (1995), *How Many People Can the Earth Support?*, London: Norton

Eurostat (1996), *Eurostat Yearbook 1996*, Luxembourg: Office for the Official Publications of the European Communities

Fitzpatrick, D. (1984), 'Irish Emigration 1801–1921', *Studies in Irish Economic and Social History*, no. 1, Economic and Social History Society of Ireland/Dundalgan Press

Fitzpatrick, D. (1985), 'Marriage in post-Famine Ireland', in A. Cosgrove (ed.), *Marriage in Ireland*, Dublin: College Press, pp. 116–131

Flinn, M.W. (1981), *The European Demographic System 1500–1820*, Brighton: Harvester Press

Guinnane, T. (1997), *The Vanishing Irish*, Princeton: Princeton University Press

Hajnal, J. (1965), 'European marriage patterns in perspective', in D.V. Glass and D.E.C. Eversley (eds.), *Population in History: Essays in Historical Demography*, London: Arnold, pp. 101–148

Hatton, T.J. and Williamson, J.G. (1994), 'What drove the mass migrations from Europe in the late nineteenth century?', *Population and Development Review*, 20(3), pp. 533–559

Kennedy, F. (1989), *Family, Economy and Government in Ireland*, ESRI General Research Series Paper No. 143, Dublin: Economic and Social Research Institute

Kennedy, K. (1975), *Population and Development. Ireland since Independence*, ESRI Reprint Series No. 41, Dublin: Economic and Social Research Institute

Lee, R.D. (1986), 'Malthus and Boserup: a dynamic synthesis', in D. Coleman and R. Schofield (eds.), *The State of Population Theory. Forward from Malthus*, Oxford: Blackwell, pp. 96–130

Livi-Bacci, M. (1997), *A Concise History of World Population*, (2nd edn), Oxford: Blackwell

Mitchell, B.R. (1992), *International Historical Statistics. Europe 1750–1988*, London: Macmillan

Mokyr, J. (1983), *Why Ireland Starved: A Quantitative and Analytical History of the Irish Economy, 1800–1850*, London: George Allen and Unwin

Mokyr, J. and Ó Gráda, C. (1982), 'Emigration and poverty in prefamine Ireland', *Explorations in Economic History 19*, pp. 360–384

Ó Gráda, C. (1989), *The Great Irish Famine*, Dublin: Gill and Macmillan

Ó Gráda, C. (1993), *Ireland Before and After the Famine*, Manchester: Manchester University Press

Ó Gráda, C. (1994), *Ireland. A New Economic History 1780–1939*, Oxford: Clarendon Press

Ó Gráda, C. (1995), 'The Great Famine and today's famines', in C. Pórtéir (ed.), *The Great Irish Famine*, Dublin: Mercier Press

Ó Gráda, C. (1997), *A Rocky Road. The Irish Economy since the 1920s*, Manchester: Manchester University Press

United Nations (1990), *Demographic Yearbook*, New York: United Nations

Vaughan, W.E. and Fitzpatrick, A.J. (1978), *Irish Historical Statistics. Population 1821–1971*, Dublin: Royal Irish Academy

Walsh, B. (1985), 'Marriage in Ireland in the twentieth century', in A. Cosgrove (ed.), *Marriage in Ireland*, Dublin: College Press, pp. 132–150

Walsh, B. (1970), 'Marriage rates and population pressure: Ireland, 1871 and 1911', *Economic History Review*, 23(1), pp. 148–162

4

Life on the Land

GEARÓID Ó TUATHAIGH

In 1847 Ireland was in the throes of the greatest social calamity in her history. The failure in successive years of the potato crop, on which more than one-third of Ireland's population of 8.5 million depended virtually exclusively for subsistence, brought about high excess mortality and massive emigration. Between 1845 and 1851 there was excess mortality of approximately one million; and emigration levels went well above one million. By 1851 the population of Ireland had fallen to 6.6 million. In the decades that followed, emigration, while heavier in some decades than in others, saw to it that the population continued to decline: by 1911 it had fallen to 4.4 million.

The calamity decimated the rural poor – the labourers, cottiers and smallholders – and the post-famine decades saw major changes take place in Irish agriculture and Irish rural society. This essay will focus on some of the key aspects of that transformation.

Rural society at the time of the Famine

Ireland in the 1840s was an overwhelmingly rural society. Agriculture was the main form of economic activity. Some five-sixths of the population of over eight million lived in the countryside (i.e. in settlements of less than 1,500 people). As domestic industry declined in the pre-famine decades, the dependence on the land for a living became even more pronounced. Belfast (in the early stage of its industrial expansion) and Dublin (a commercial and administrative capital) were the only expanding urban centres; most other towns by the 1840s were either stagnating or becoming bloated with an influx of the unemployed rural poor.

In a pre-electric age, darkness was a stark reality of life after sunset. An acute sense of sound and smell mattered. Candles, rushes and oil-lamps lit the houses of the better off, and everywhere in the countryside there was the smell of turf, the abundant supply of which provided fuel for some one million families. Farmyard animals – including the ubiquitous pig – regularly sheltered under the same roof as the cottier or smallholder, and manure and dung lay in the door of many small cabins. However, as these were important economic resources: poor hygiene did not necessarily mean abject poverty.

Some 15 million acres of agricultural land was cultivated in the 1840s, of which more than one-third was under tillage and potatoes. Though cattle numbers and exports were rising, tillage items accounted for 60 per cent of total output in the early 1840s. Allowing for regional variations, there was an impressive grid of markets and fairs for agricultural produce; a high and growing volume of agricultural exports (overwhelmingly to Britain); and evidence of improvements (in livestock, grain and potato strains) among the progressive and more commercially-minded producers. Though 'backward' in some respects when compared to English agriculture, Irish agriculture showed clear signs of expansion and growth (in output and in exports) and increased commercialisation in the pre-famine decades.

Of course, there was another side to this story. The huge tillage sector was supported by an army of cheap labour and by the price support of the corn laws. For a large proportion of the rural society (perhaps as many as 40 per cent) their economy was at subsistence level, based on potato cultivation and consumption, with their labour sold (in a saturated labour market) for access to potato plots. The collapse (under increasing pressure from machine-made cloth and clothing) of the domestic textile industry in the pre-famine period deepened rural poverty, not least among the increasingly high quota of unemployed women.

Irish rural society presented a picture of marked contrasts. Most of the land was owned by, at most, about 10,000 landlords, though many of these had relatively small estates. As proprietors they were a mixed bag: some conscientious, competent and caring; others incompetent, profligate and uncaring. Among landlords, absenteeism was most prevalent on the poorer land of the more remote areas of Connacht and Ulster. Between 20 per cent and 30 per cent of the land was owned by landlords resident outside Ireland. At the bottom of the social pyramid was a vast army of landless or virtually landless male rural labourers, perhaps more than a million, with a further 300,000 male cottiers on holdings of less than five acres. This left about 250,000 family farmers with mean holdings of about twenty acres, and a further 100,000 with a mean of fifty acres. Finally, about 50,000 farmers, with mean holdings of about eighty acres, could be considered well off.

The contrasts between the well off and the poorer classes were evident in every aspect of their living standards. In housing, some 40 per cent of the rural population lived in one-room cabins or tenements (many of these cabins no better than a mud-based lean-to at the edge of a bog). Clothing was thin and threadbare for this rural proletariat. Their diet, if nutritional, was monotonous, with potatoes as the staple regularly combined with buttermilk. As one moved up the social ladder, housing improved, as did clothing; while a more varied diet increasingly included tea and sugar in addition to bread, even for the more frugal family farmers. Literacy rates also reflected these social cleavages in rural society. If religion offered comfort in adversity and promoted social cohesion (at least within denominations), rural social tensions, from a great variety of sources, frequently exploded into violence (though state systems of elementary education and of policing were beginning to have an impact on rural society from the 1840s).

The shift from tillage to pasture

The Famine decimated the poorer classes of rural Ireland. In the crisis years the number of labourers and cottiers was almost halved, the number of farms less than fifteen acres fell by more than one-third. The social structure of rural Ireland was brutally reshaped. Debt and insolvency forced many landlords to sell property in the immediate aftermath of the Famine. In the decades between 1851 and 1914, the restructuring of Irish rural society continued, driven by two principal and related developments: the decline in population numbers and the long-term shift from tillage to pasture in Irish agriculture. Emigration drew off thousands from the land – disproportionately from the lower end of the social ladder. The overall population fell to 4.4 million in 1911; the proportion living in rural Ireland fell from five-sixths to two-thirds in the seventy years after 1847.

Cattle and dairying eclipsed tillage in the rural economy: between the 1850s and 1914 cattle numbers rose by a third, the acreage under hay by 75 per cent, while the acreage under grain fell by 50 per cent. The total number of farms fell by 15 per cent, but average farm size increased. In short, the comfortable farming group consolidated their position and came to predominate in many aspects of rural society – from marriage patterns to religious behaviour, in political movements as in general social values. Perhaps the most significant victory of the comfortable tenant-farmers came with the land war and its aftermath. During a downturn in agricultural incomes the tenant-farmers combined to challenge the landlords, initially with a view to gaining better terms within their tenancy (the so-called three Fs: fair rents, fixity of tenure, and freedom to sell the tenant's 'interest' in the farm). But the intervention of the government, in arbitrating (through a land commission) on disputed claims, proved so demoralising to the landlords that eventually it was decided that the best solution was for the government to provide the funds to encourage the landlords to sell the farms to the occupiers and to enable the farmers to buy. After a slow start, the favourable terms of the Wyndham Act of 1903 (with later amendments) finally persuaded the farmers of Ireland to begin availing of the government loans to buy out their farms. In 1870 as few as 3 per cent of the occupiers of Irish farms actually owned the farms, by 1914 over 60 per cent were already owners or were on their way to becoming owners. This figure continued to rise after the Free State government resumed estate-land acquisition and distribution in the independent Irish state from 1923 forward.

With modestly-rising productivity in an increasingly pastoral agricultural economy, and (allowing for occasional set-backs) with farmers sharing in long-term real increases in agricultural incomes, living standards for the declining population of rural Ireland generally improved in the decades from 1851 to 1920. Bank and post-office deposits, higher and more varied consumption patterns (in food, dress, household utensils and general comforts), increases in passenger and freight traffic on the railway network, all testify to this improvement. Increasing commercialisation was reflected in the growing number of commercial travellers, in more organised markets, and in the emergence of large stores in major rural towns.

Apart from the decisive shift from tillage to pasture, there was significant innovation (in strains of cattle and crops) among progressive farmers, together with increasing mechanisation from the mid-century: for example, reaping, mowing, threshing and potato-spraying machines, and, with the rise in creameries from the 1890s: the milk-separator.

It is probably fair to say that all classes shared, though in different degrees, in this rising tide of rural prosperity in the later nineteenth and early twentieth century. Even the agricultural labourer improved his lot. True, the number of agricultural labourers fell dramatically, from approximately 350,000 as late as 1880 to 160,000 by 1930 and further to around 80,000 by 1955; but at the turn of the century, the labourers' real wages were rising. Government intervention produced a programme of labourers' cottages (each with an acre of ground attached from the 1890s). Some 54,000 cottages had been built by 1923. The labourers' diet and dress also improved, at least in terms of variety. As John Boyle has remarked of the labourer's diet at this time, with 'bread and tea, he also had eggs and milk when they were plentiful, 'yalla male' as a standby, and at times meat in the shape of American salt bacon ...'. He regularly smoked his pipe and his children were better clothed (while still usually barefoot) than ever before, though there undoubtedly remained pockets of deep rural poverty well into the present century. Further up the social ladder, the improvements in housing and dress, greater variety in diet and, as time went on, household utensils and creature comforts, were enjoyed pro rata with size and quality of farm and farm income.

These increased comforts, however, did not halt the flow of emigration among labourers, any more than did the interventions of the state's Congested Districts Board among poor 'congested' smallholders in the western counties from the 1890s. Rural Ireland became more prosperous as it became less populated. Emigrants' remittances contributed to the comforts of those who remained. Horace Plunkett's Co-operative Movement along with the establishment of a Department of Agriculture and Technical Instruction in 1899 added to the overall improvements in Irish agriculture and in rural living standards in the years before 1914. No wonder, then, that Irish farmers responded sharply to the buoyant demand and price boom for agricultural produce in Britain during the years of the Great War (1914–18).

Independence

Whatever high hopes Irish nationalists may have expressed on what could be achieved by independence, the first four decades of the Irish Free State were, on the whole, difficult and disappointing for Irish agriculture. The Cumann na nGaedheal governments of the 1920s, initially faced with a sharp fall in agricultural prices in the post-war years, sought to encourage profitability and efficiency in agriculture within the traditional free-trade corridor to the low-priced UK market. Fianna Fáil's ardent protectionism envisaged self-sufficiency in food, but it also had more explicitly social aims in its agricultural policy, seeking as it did to settle as many farm families as possible in reasonable comfort on the land. In practical terms, this meant a renewed effort at further land redistribution and a drive towards increased tillage and more balanced land use.

But, while incentives in the 1930s and compulsion during the war years secured a temporary expansion in tillage acreage, there was to be no reversal of long-established trends. Pasture resumed its sway after 1945, and the small farmers continued leaving the land and heading to the cities of North America and, increasingly from the 1930s, to Britain. Indeed, the bruising tariff war with Britain in the 1930s inflicted severe damage on Irish agricultural output, exports and incomes; damage from which recovery was slow. In fact, the economic stagnation and social torpor of the 1950s prompted the most severe haemorrhage of emigrants out of Ireland for almost a century, with over 400,000 leaving in the crisis decade. The western counties, in particular, seemed to be decanting their rural population at an alarming rate. Community leaders, bishops and social commentators spoke of 'the vanishing Irish', warned of a 'dying rural society', and called for urgent action to 'save the West'.

Even among those who hung on, the burden of history seemed to lie heavy on many of them. The obsessive urge to possess *The Field* is terrifyingly illustrated in John B. Keane's Bull McCabe. Likewise, the pattern of delayed marriages, life-long celibacy and high quotas of ageing bachelors and spinsters, which the need to secure undivided inheritance had imposed on sections of rural society, exacted a high price on the human spirit. The tragic portrait of Patrick Maguire, in Kavanagh's *The Great Hunger*, is a grim reminder of the price sometimes paid for holding on.

The story of these decades, however, is not all gloom and doom. The difficulties of the small farmers produced brave, if short-lived, political challenge (in Clann na Talmhan). A clutch of voluntary organisations brought energy and enthusiasm to the task of improving living standards, morale and the quality of social life in rural communities. These included the Irish Countrywomen's Association, Muintir na Tíre and Macra na Feirme, from the latter of which emerged in the early 1950s the Irish Creamery Milk Suppliers' Association and the NFA (now the Irish Farmers' Association), the key organisations in the very effective farming 'lobby' of recent decades. The churches offered solace, consolation and discipline, and some church leaders championed action and agitation in the cause of rural renewal. Likewise, the Gaelic Athletic Association, based on the parish club, bonded local communities in loyalty and pride, and provided great social gatherings on match Sundays, though it could not stay the haemorrhage from rural Ireland.

The spread of new machinery (notably tractors) continued steadily, relative to farm size. However, there was one notable advance in technology that had a profound impact on domestic and social life in rural Ireland in the three decades after 1945: the great project of rural electrification. With electrification came labour-saving devices in farm work (including, in time, milking machines), changes in reading habits and forms of entertainment (at home and in public places), the plugged-in radio and in the early 1960s: the television. These and other benefits of electrification transformed many aspects of rural life and contributed hugely to changes in outlook and attitude within the rural community in recent decades.

It would be difficult to exaggerate the impact of these social changes: aspirations, expectations and consciousness of alternative ways and possibilities of seeing and doing things, were all affected by the complex impact of the changing communications environment. In time, technology would convince many that rural living need not and, in fact, did not involve isolation from currents of ideas and culture circulating in the world beyond the village or townland. In time, so far as the flow of ideas and information was concerned, the global village of the communications age would embrace the remote rural valley as well as the urban main street.

But in the short term, in a depressed economy and with the strong urge to seize opportunity and greater personal freedom drawing Irish emigrants to the bright lights of London or New York, such social improvements as occurred in the immediate post-war years failed to halt the flight from the snipe-grass during the 1950s.

The Common Agricultural Policy

By 1960 Irish agriculture was in a poor condition. Farm incomes were low by West European standards and agricultural exports were going overwhelmingly to the competitive and low-priced UK market. But farm incomes would have been much lower were it not for significant state aid to farmers throughout the 1960s. By 1972 about one-third of the farmers' income came from various state supports. Not surprisingly, hopes were high that there would be a dramatic improvement following Ireland's entry to the European Economic Community (EEC) in 1973. The EEC meant higher, and guaranteed, prices for most Irish farm products, together with various capital grants and supports for underdeveloped areas. Apart from a sharp price drop in 1974, the early years of Ireland's EEC membership did indeed bring a significant rise in prices for Irish farm produce. As the Common Agricultural Policy (CAP) supported the price of produce, the more commercially advanced and prosperous farmers did better than the smaller farmers with more limited potential (in land or capital) for increased output. The gap in prosperity between the commercially-viable farmers and the struggling smallholders widened and the number of small farmers continued to decline.

Since the late 1970s, however, the situation regarding incomes has been more unstable, even for the more commercial farmers. The moves towards a more liberal global market for agricultural produce, and the reform of the European CAP, have transformed the prospects for Irish farming. A more regulatory regime has developed in Brussels, which seeks to control and manage agricultural production, in quantity and in quality. For many products, price supports have given way to quotas and other restrictions on production. It is a far cry from the 1847 potato plots, on stony hillsides, several hundred feet above sea level, to the 1997 policy of financial compensation for land 'set-aside' from production, monitored from the sky by satellite pictures.

Moreover, apart from reducing the volume of agricultural production, the current direction of European agricultural policy is increasingly conscious of consumer taste and demand, in respect of standards, hygiene and safety (as the crisis in demand for beef following the BSE outbreak has powerfully demonstrated). Traceability and certification in the food chain is increasingly the demand of health-conscious consumers. Irish farmers, as producers, must respond to these new consumer-oriented policies. Changes in the structure of the food-processing industry, and in the structure of the wholesale and retail food business – changes which have seen the growth to a dominant position of a small number of giant combines in these sectors – will also have implications for the particular demands (in quantity, in product range and in quality) for Irish farm produce.

Diversification of socio-economic activity

But the future of rural society in Ireland raises questions that go beyond the prospects for Irish agriculture. There are other profound social changes taking place that will make it increasingly difficult to speak of the rural community and the farming community as if they were synonymous. Increased mobility, together with the complex impact of information technology on employment prospects and patterns – particularly in the service industries (for example, telecottages) – continue to facilitate lifestyle choices that would have been unthinkable a generation ago. An increasing number of gainfully-employed people may decide – for environmental and social reasons – to live in a relatively dispersed settlement in the countryside, while having virtually no contact (apart from their own vegetable garden) with farming as we have traditionally known it.

There is a further dimension to the diversification of economic activity, interest and income for sections of the rural community in our own time. In a world conscious of the global dangers to the environment, policy-makers at national and European level are increasingly articulating a view of rural dwellers as being responsible managers of a precious resource: the land. Within a vulnerable eco-system, rural society is seen as having a vital custodial function, for which it must be appropriately rewarded. This particular view will call for a radical reorientation of attitudes and will have profound implications for education among all sections of our population.

Rural Ireland today bears little resemblance to the landed community of 1847. Certainly, pockets of poverty and, more commonly, of relative social deprivation still exist today in rural Ireland, especially at a distance from the larger towns and cities. But this cannot be compared to the teeming army of the poor in the congested rural Ireland of 1847. The surviving big houses of the landlords are nowadays likely to be hotels, nursing homes or the status homes of the new rich – the superstars of business or of the entertainment industry. The extensive private land parks of the old landlord class have been replaced by the luxury golf and leisure clubs of the new entrepreneurs of the tourist and leisure business. Within commuting distance of our major towns and cities, a field is more valuable as a site for a house than under crops or cattle. Political controversy now centres on planning and zoning issues rather than on the law of landlord-tenant relations.

The farm labourer has all but passed into history and folklore; the struggling smallholder seems destined to follow before too long. Technology and labour-saving machinery have transformed the work-routine – and the prospects for leisure-time – of the comfortable, economically-viable sectors of the farming community. Back-breaking toil on small or fragmented holdings may still be the lot of a diminishing band of marginal smallholders, but it is unlikely to be taken up by their children, in an expanding economy with diverse educational and occupational opportunities and in a society which places a high premium on gratification and leisure. Television and video in better-insulated and brighter farm houses may not be sufficient to halt the continuing drift out of farming from the ranks of the struggling smallholders.

In summary, as we approach the end of the millennium, the Irish countryside is a very different human habitat to that which experienced the horrors of the Famine 150 years ago. The economic basis of Irish agriculture has changed significantly and continues to change in a competitive global market where, at least in the developed world, the political balance now favours consumers more than producers. Consumers, moreover, with high demands of convenience, health, hygiene and safety in their choice of food. Current trends suggest a future in which fewer rural dwellers will be engaged in producing primary agricultural products. More farm families will be required to put together an acceptable income from a mixture of profitable activities (a process already well-advanced in rural Ireland), such as niche production of traceable, environmentally-safe food; agri-tourism; and financial reward for responsible land-management (including forestry, whatever doubts may persist as to its 'antisocial' logic) on broad environmental grounds.

The wonder of the countryside and of nature will continue to fascinate and to excite respect. But the humans who share that habitat with plants and animals will be very different in their economic activity, in their social habits, in their lifestyle and attitudes from their forebears, who were the first 'sample' communities for the interest and expertise of the pioneering statisticians who founded the Dublin Statistical Society 150 years ago.

FURTHER READING

Aalen, F.H.A., Whelan, K. and Stout, M. (eds.) (1997), *Atlas of the Irish Rural Landscape*, Cork: Cork University Press

Central Statistics Office (1997), *Farming since the Famine: Irish Farm Statistics 1847–1996*, Dublin: Stationery Office

Clark, S. and Donnelly Jr, J. (eds.) (1983), *Irish Peasants: Violence and Political Unrest 1780–1914*, Dublin: Gill and Macmillan

Drudy, P.J. (ed.) (1982), *Ireland: Land, Politics and People*, Cambridge: Cambridge University Press

Hannan, D. (1970), *Rural Exodus: a study of the forces influencing the large-scale migration of Irish rural youth*, London: Geoffrey Chapman

Kennedy, K.A., Giblin, T. and McHugh, D. (1988), *The economic development of Ireland in the twentieth century*, London and New York: Routledge

Lee, J.J. (1989), *Ireland 1912–1985: Politics and Society*, Cambridge: Cambridge University Press

NESC (1994), *New Approaches to Rural Development*, NESC Report No. 97

Ó Gráda, C. (1988), *Ireland before and after the Famine*, Manchester: Manchester University Press

5

Health, Housing and Social Welfare

MIRIAM M. WILEY

Any review of developments in the health, housing and social welfare systems over the past century and a half must logically extend back to 1838. With the enactment of the Irish Poor Law in that year, the roots of our health and welfare systems were firmly sown. As we attempt to trace how these systems have grown since then, we must focus on the highlights of this history, rather than provide a detailed account of specific developments over the past 150 years.

The Poor Law system

The introduction of the Irish Poor Law in 1838 was a response to the increasing level of destitution in Ireland. The implementation of this legislation involved the division of the country into administrative areas called 'unions', each of which had to provide a workhouse for the provision of relief to the destitute poor. The application of the workhouse test meant that relief could only be provided within the workhouse, where living conditions were deliberately kept at the lowest possible levels with the intention of deterring all but the most destitute from seeking relief. Important features of this fledgling welfare system have prevailed in varying degrees through the century and a half following enactment, including the fact that the granting of relief was contingent on the recipients themselves proving to be part of the so-called 'deserving' poor. Establishing eligibility for relief has continued to be part of subsequent social welfare schemes which may be targeted towards specific categories of recipients, such as the elderly or widows and orphans.

A catastrophic event like the Famine of 1845–47 was inevitably going to bring enormous pressure to bear on a system as inadequate as that introduced with the 1838 Poor Law. The huge increase in the number of poor, destitute and starving people proved beyond the capacity of the workhouse system. In response to this crisis, the government in 1847 was forced to introduce a system of outdoor relief, which involved the provision of relief to the poor outside the workhouse. While originally made available to limited groups, this provision for outdoor relief was the beginning of the home assistance scheme. This scheme operated in different forms until 1977 when it was replaced by the supplementary welfare allowance scheme.[1] Though amended and modified over time, the system put in place by the Poor Law became the touchstone by which subsequent state provision for different categories of need was assessed.

The development of the social welfare system

In reviewing particularly critical points in the development of the social welfare system, the Workmen's Compensation Act 1897 marked an important departure because, for the first time, defined groups of the employed were given a right to benefit in specified circumstances. Those aged over seventy were the group targeted by the Old Age Pension Act 1908. The provision of case payments to this group was subject to a means test rather than a test of destitution, which again was considered a major advance. The introduction of the National Insurance Act in 1911 was important in marking the start of the first compulsory social insurance scheme. The provision of unemployment benefit and sickness benefit under a compulsory insurance scheme involved a 'kind of contractual relationship between the insured and the State' and was a significant departure from the discretionary benevolence which was at the heart of the old Poor Law system.[2] The unemployed who were outside of the insurance net had to wait until 1933 before unemployment assistance was introduced – in response to the big increase in hardship following the world economic depression after 1929. Statutory provision was also made for the blind, widows and orphans, and children in the first half of the twentieth century with the introduction of the Blind Person's Pension in 1920, Widow's and Orphan's Pensions in 1935 and Children's Allowance in 1944.

The Department of Social Welfare was established in 1947 and in the following decade the social insurance system was consolidated and a basis for future initiatives established. While a number of groups benefited from these initiatives, the broadest range of provision through the 1960s was directed at the elderly. The decade began with the introduction of the old-age contributory pension in 1961 and in 1967 free travel was introduced, followed soon after by allowances for such commodities as electricity and the television licence and the availability of retirement and invalidity pensions in 1970.

Through the 1970s, however, there was a growing awareness of the importance of responding to the needs of women. This concern was marked by the publication of the *Report of the Commission on the Status of Women* in 1972, which made a number of recommendations aimed at ensuring equality of treatment for women under the social welfare code. The 1970s saw the introduction of provisions aimed specifically at women in particular circumstances, including the Deserted Wife's Allowance and Benefit in 1970 and 1973 respectively, Unmarried Mother's Allowance in 1973, and the Single Woman's Allowance and the Prisoner's Wife's Allowance in 1974. It was in 1978, however, that an EEC directive calling for equality of treatment between men and women in matters of social security was adopted by the Council of Ministers. As the main areas of discrimination in the Irish system concerned the treatment of married women, it was not until the enactment of legislation in 1985 that the removal of this discrimination was addressed.[3] A more family orientation could be said to characterise initiatives in the 1980s, which included the introduction of the Maternity Allowance in 1981 and Family Income Supplement in 1984.

The introduction of pay-related benefit in 1974 and pay-related social insurance in 1979 were important advances on the social insurance scheme introduced at the beginning of this century as, for the first time, ability to pay was taken into account. Under the pay-related social insurance system the differentials that had formerly existed between men and women, and between those in agriculture and in other occupations, were finally eliminated.

Health service provision

In switching our focus to the development of health service provision from the mid-nineteenth century, the 1838 Poor Law is again the logical starting point. By confining the destitute poor in workhouses throughout the country, the authorities had to provide health, as well as social, services for the inhabitants. The recurring outbreaks of infectious diseases at this time gave additional impetus to the expansion of the state's involvement in the provision of medical services. The lethal epidemics of the Famine, together with the appalling death rates, resulted in the enactment of the Medical Charities Act in 1851.[4] Under this legislation, the dispensary system that had been developing nationally was targeted for expansion. Each Poor Law union was divided into dispensary districts and commissioners were given responsibility for the availability of dispensaries and medical officers within these districts. These dispensary doctors were employed on a salaried basis to attend the sick poor in the district. A perspective on the medical profession's view of the dispensary system can be gathered from the comment by Dr E.D. Mapother, a medical officer in the 1860s, that there were many difficulties with the system, 'for instance, it would be lamentable that a brilliant man should be wasted on a dismal western district'.[5] We would, however, have to assume that this was not a generalised view as the dispensary system continued to operate for 120 years up to the 1970s.[6]

While significant scientific discoveries had advanced the practice of medicine in the nineteenth century, the most substantial challenges were still posed by attempts to prevent and contain outbreaks of infectious diseases. Improved sanitation, however, rather than the expansion of medical services, was to constitute an important factor in meeting these challenges. With the passing of the Public Health Act in 1878, public authorities were given power to destroy unsound food, supervise slaughterhouses and isolate persons with notifiable infectious diseases like typhus and cholera. Improvements in public sanitation had a big impact on reducing the death rate from the principal epidemic diseases of the time, including smallpox, typhus fever, typhoid, measles, diphtheria, whooping cough, scarlet fever and diarrhoea.

The struggle with tuberculosis, the most common cause of death among Irish people at the turn of this century, is an important part of the story of the development of the Irish health services. Despite accounting for more than 11,500 deaths per year in the early 1900s, tuberculosis was not a notifiable infectious disease under public legislation. The disease was associated with poverty, poor diet and bad housing and there was an erroneous perception that a family weakness caused susceptibility to the disease. Accordingly, people tried to conceal the problem, resulting in a general sense of apathy to its management. Although the disease became notifiable in the 1920s,[7] the economic difficulties of the time actually led to a reduction of the limited services available for sufferers, rather than the expansion warranted by the scale of the disease among the Irish population. It was not until the 1930s – when an upturn in the death rate from this disease in Ireland contrasted with the downward trend in other European countries – that the scale of investment in the required services began to be recognised. The campaign to combat TB gathered momentum in the early 1940s and by 1945 legislation brought the widespread provision of sanitoria, which were free to all, irrespective of income.[8] Through the 1940s and early 1950s there were big increases in the number of sanitoria beds and services available to TB sufferers. A national blood transfusion service became available in 1948, extensive vaccination with BCG was begun in 1949 and streptomycin was in effective use from 1950 onwards. The effectiveness of this concerted campaign was significant, with death rates from TB being more than halved in the seven years after 1945.[9]

Funding of health services

The framework of the national health service system imposed by the Poor Law structure was maintained until after the founding of the Irish Free State. With the establishment of the Department of Local Government and Public Health in 1924, the county became the principal administrative unit for poor relief and health care. The consolidation of responsibility for the health services within local health authorities continued until 1947 when the Department of Health was established. While the dispensary service was more concerned with the delivery of care by general practitioners based in the community and was considered more of a local responsibility, the provision of hospital services gradually became a charge on central government. Many of our voluntary hospitals originated as charitable institutions in the eighteenth century, including the Charitable Infirmary, Jervis Street (1718), Dr Steevens' Hospital (1720), Mercer's Hospital and the Rotunda (1745) and the Meath Hospital (1753). The expansion of the voluntary hospital system continued in the nineteenth century with the establishment of the Coombe in the 1820s and in 1834 the Adelaide was founded for the purpose of catering for Protestant patients.[10] Also in 1834, St Vincent's became the first hospital to be organised and staffed by women, the Mercy Hospital in Cork was established in 1857, the Mater Hospital was founded on Dublin's northside in 1861, and the National Maternity Hospital, Holles Street dates back to 1894.[11] With the exception of Jervis Street, Dr Steevens' and Mercer's, the remaining hospitals, which are all over 100 years old, continue to serve the sick today.

The establishment of such notable hospitals in the eighteenth and nineteenth centuries was a significant achievement, but by the early twentieth century voluntary hospital development was in danger of collapsing due to lack of funds. In response to this funding crisis, legislation passed in 1931 ensured that proceeds from the Hospital Sweepstakes would be used to fund hospitals. In addition, the establishment of a Hospitals Commission in 1933 recognised the need for the centralised control over the development of the Irish hospital system that has continued to the present time.

The 1940s saw a period of intense debate over the future shape of the Irish health service system. As many European countries were expanding the insurance basis for their health systems, and Britain was on the verge of introducing a national health service, the possibilities offered by both options had to be seriously considered in the Irish context. The result was that neither option was fully adopted and so the Health Act of 1947 was to lay the foundations for a peculiarly Irish system – incorporating elements of several models. This Act marked a significant increase in state involvement in the health services. Universal free services had been rejected in favour of providing specified services to pre-defined groups on a nominal or no-charge basis, with the rest of the population deemed fit to pay for their own health care.

This period is, of course, also noteworthy for the failure of Dr Noel Browne's proposed reorganisation of services for mothers and children because of opposition from the Catholic hierarchy and the medical profession. One commentary on the implications of this triangular conflict – between the church, the medical profession and the state – concludes that an important implication was 'to enshrine means tests or income tests as determinants of many services'.[12] According to the hierarchy, means tests were the method of determining where public responsibility for health ended and where individual and family responsibility began. Barrington (1987) concludes that this conflict was seen to encourage an 'extraordinary symbiosis of public and private medicine', which continues to characterise the Irish health services of today.

A modified mother and child scheme providing maternity services for some women and a comprehensive medical service for their infants was introduced with the Health Act of 1953. This Act also finalised the transfer of the dispensary system to the local health authorities and broadened access to hospital services. An important advancement of this legislation was the replacement of the unpalatable individual means test by the statutory recognition of the general groups eligible for defined services.[13] Following this legislation, the statutory health services seemed to offer little to the population in the upper income group. In order to facilitate this group in insuring against the costs of catastrophic illness, the state-sponsored Voluntary Health Insurance Board was established in 1957 to provide voluntary health insurance on a not-for-profit basis.

As the demands of the health services expanded throughout the 1950s and 1960s and the local rates proved to be an inadequate funding source, the central health authorities assumed a greater proportion of the increased costs. A White Paper in 1966 finally proposed that ultimate responsibility for health service financing should rest with the state. It was recognised that such a shift of responsibility would also warrant changes in the administration of the services and these were given effect in the Health Act of 1970. The local authority base for health service administration was replaced with the framework of eight regional health boards that continues to operate today. The demands of a modern health care system needed a structure spanning county boundaries to provide facilities which could be supported by a substantial concentration of population. The dispensary system that had been put in place in 1851 was finally replaced by the General Medical Service in 1972. While a means test to determine eligibility for free general practitioner care was retained within the new system, patients were accorded the right to choose their doctor and pharmacist, thereby avoiding the stigma long-associated with attendance at the dispensary.

Housing

The relationship between standards of health and housing has long been recognised. As early as 1880, in an address to the thirty-fourth session of the Statistical and Social Inquiry Society of Ireland, the Society's president made the following statement:

> The health of our poorer people is lowered in greatest degree by wretchedness of habitation. In 1871 there were in Ireland 155,000 one roomed cabins, with an average of four inmates ... Such hovels are often pitched regardless of dryness of soil, or means of approach; their clay floors are soaked with organic matter, or hollowed into pools; their roofs are of decomposing straw, or rushes; they are often without back doors, or movable windows for airing; and their chimneys are so ill built that smoke fills the dwellings in windy weather – hence ophthalmia used to be a constant

> Irish pest, but somehow it has lessened, and the girls have better complexions than the smoked ham ...[14]

While not commenting on the complexion of the inhabitants, a report specific to the capital city at the turn of the century suggests that 'Dublin was notorious for its poverty, appalling tenements, filthy streets, high death rate and the lack of interest of its citizens in preventive health'.[15] Given the connections between poverty, sanitation and life expectancy, the standard of housing is clearly an important factor in the welfare of any society. The desolation caused by the institutional basis of the workhouse system, which made relief contingent on people giving up their own personal dwelling, shows the importance of a 'sense of place' for the Irish. There were some legislative attempts in the late nineteenth century to address housing needs, including legislation in 1860 enabling landlords to borrow for the provision of cottages in rural areas, though 1890 marks the first serious attempt to deal with the problems of urban housing and slum clearance. It is interesting that as far back as 1899 the facility provided to local authorities to grant loans for house purchase was already setting the trend for high rates of owner-occupation, which continues to be an important characteristic of Irish society today. This trend was further strengthened in 1919 when the Housing Act initiated a policy of state aid for house purchase, which still prevails in a variety of ways.

The founding of the Free State saw the launch of the 'Million Pound Scheme' aimed at generating substantial up-front investment for a large-scale building initiative. It was not until the 1930s that the main drive at slum clearance was undertaken. Between 1932 and 1942, 82,000 new dwellings were built, while 11,000 condemned houses were demolished.[16] The post-war period, however, saw a dramatic fall in the rate of house building, while the need for rehousing continued to rise. To address this problem, legislation in the late 1940s again tried to encourage the growing rate of owner-occupation by granting higher loans to house purchasers and expanding local authorities' powers to address special housing problems. While house building increased as a result, the downward trend was again resumed in the late 1950s when emigration was high and capital expenditure on housing by local authorities was significantly reduced. The improvement in economic growth in the 1960s was associated with increased investment by local authorities and it was at this time that developments such as Ballymun, one of the largest single housing projects in Europe, were initiated.

In attempting to understand why the Irish level of owner-occupation is one of the highest in Europe, one commentator from the 1960s concluded:

> The typical Irishman prefers not to live in a flat but in a house ... and if the opportunity can be had, he prefers the option of owning the land to renting it. In this history-minded country, the past centuries of eviction and forced emigration have left their mark on the housing system ... The absence of the excessive problems of urbanisation allied with the predominantly rural-based population have been important influences on the housing system, making ownership rather than tenancy the norm.[17]

The level of owner-occupation in Ireland has continued to grow in recent decades, rising from a level of 53 per cent in 1946 to almost 80 per cent in 1991. In acknowledging that housing is a basic need and not just an optional extra, recent housing legislation requires each local authority to periodically assess the need for adequate and suitable housing accommodation. The range of initiatives covered by the 1988 Housing Act is also indicative of a recognition of the importance of greater diversification in responding to the more complex nature of housing need observed in contemporary society.[18]

Conclusion

Irish society today has come a long way from the 'mud-housed, rag-clad, potato-fed' race described by Thomas Carlyle in 1840.[19] While close to 100 out of every 1,000 babies born in the 1880s died before their first birthday, in the Ireland of the 1990s all but around 6 out of every 1,000 babies born can expect to live beyond this milestone. Babies born at the beginning of this decade can now expect to live into their seventies while those born in the 1920s could only expect to live into their late fifties. The development of our health, housing and social welfare systems over the century and a half since the dark and desolate days of the Poor Law, has been significantly influenced by the state of the economy as a whole. While the achievements of these systems in Ireland are now on a par with those of our European neighbours, much still remains to be done if we are to ensure that all our citizens enjoy acceptable living, health and housing standards. As we approach the dawn of a new millennium, it is to be hoped that the recent improvements in the Irish economy will in the future be reflected in the way the most vulnerable members of our society are assisted in meeting these essential needs.

NOTES

1 Burke, H. (1987), *The Poor and the Poor Law in 19th Century Ireland*, England: The Women's Education Bureau

2 Marshall, T.M. (1975), *Social Policy in the Twentieth Century*, London, p. 55

3 Social Welfare (Amendment) (No. 2) Act, 1985

4 Hensey, B. (1959), *The Health Services of Ireland*, (1st edn), Dublin: Institute of Public Administration

5 Mapother, E.D. (1881), 'Address at the Opening of the Thirty-Fourth Session of the Statistical and Social Inquiry Society of Ireland', *Journal of the Statistical and Social Inquiry Society of Ireland*, January 1881, p. 101

6 Barrington, R. (1987), *Health, Medicine and Politics in Ireland 1900–1970*, Dublin: Institute of Public Administration

7 The Local Government Act, 1925

8 The Tuberculosis (Establishment of Sanitoria) Act, 1945

9 Barrington, ibid.

10 Robins, J.A. (1960), 'The Irish Hospital. An Outline of its Origins and Development', *Administration*, vol. 8, no. 2, Dublin: Institute of Public Administration

11 Fleetwood, J. (1951), *History of Medicine in Ireland*, Dublin: Browne and Nolan Limited

12 Barrington, ibid., p. 285

13 Hensey, B. (1979), *The Health Services of Ireland*, (3rd edition), Dublin: Institute of Public Administration

14 Mapother, ibid., p. 90

15 Barrington, ibid., p. 14

16 Curry, J. (1980), *The Irish Social Services*, Dublin: Institute of Public Administration

17 Pfretzschner, P. (1965), *The Dynamics of Irish Housing*, Dublin: Institute of Public Administration, p. 112

18 Fahy, T. and Watson, D. (1995), *An Analysis of Social Housing Need*, ESRI General Research Series Paper No. 168, Dublin: Economic and Social Research Institute

19 Mapother, ibid., p. 93

6

Education, Economy and Society

J.J. LEE

Education plays a central role in social and economic affairs nowadays. It enjoys a high public profile, with its own regular newspaper columns, weekly supplements, radio and television programmes. It is widely credited with making a major contribution to the emergence of the Celtic Tiger, a beast recently roused from its slumbers and now stalking the economic jungle with a vengeance. The Department of Education and Science is a big spender, and the portfolio has grown dramatically in importance in the past decade. The main challenges confronting education are not distant abstractions for the majority of citizens. They affect nearly every home in the country. The fact, for instance, that early school leavers suffer disproportionately high unemployment is rightly causing intense concern about the consequences for young people of failing to achieve minimum educational standards, thus potentially condemning themselves to a life of impoverishment, if not of crime. And every parent with a child at leaving certificate stage will have views on the points system. Educational issues, in short, lie at the very centre of the type of society we want to be.

The nineteenth century

It was very different 150 years ago. Education was the last thing on the minds of the vast majority of the Irish people in 1847, with the very survival of so many still threatened by the calamity of the Great Famine. Those who could afford the luxury of thinking about education didn't yet have a great deal to think about. The national school system had been instituted, it is true, in 1831, and was gradually supplanting the earlier hedge school system. But attendance was not compulsory, and it would not be until the twentieth century that it would become universal. There was only a thin sliver of second-level schools. Were it not for the work of religious orders, particularly the Christian Brothers, and the Presentation and Mercy Nuns, there would have been few prospects indeed for the poorer classes.

There was only one university in the country: Trinity College, Dublin – which was concerned mainly with the education of Anglican clergymen; although an 1845 Act of Sir Robert Peel's government had just established Queen's Colleges in Cork, Galway and Belfast. The Cork and Galway colleges would be combined under the 1908 University Act with University College Dublin – which emerged through various institutional vicissitudes stretching back to Newman's Catholic University in 1854 – to constitute the National University of Ireland; with which St Patrick's Maynooth, established since 1795 as a Catholic seminary, would be associated. Queen's College Belfast became a university in its own right. That 1908 Act would not be superseded until the University Act of 1997.

Bitter debates raged about education at all levels in the nineteenth century. But these were less about education in the sense of the quality of the curriculum, or the quality of teaching, than about power and control, and particularly about the relative influence of the state and the churches.

This was quite normal at the time. It was much the same all over Britain, Europe and North America. Religious belief was a powerful constituent of identity, and many of the great political battles of the nineteenth century, not least in France and Germany, revolved around the control of education. Ireland was in no way exceptional. The issue was exacerbated here, however, because religious rivalry was so key a factor in the war of identities between Irish and British nationalism, which ensured an added injection of vitriol into the conflicting claims of the churches.

The national school system established in 1831 was originally intended to be non-denominational. No church was satisfied with this, and the system gradually became denominational. In practice, most schools would probably have been denominational anyway, particularly in the west and south of Ireland, which were overwhelmingly Catholic. In fact, denominational schooling was widespread in the nineteenth-century European and American world. However, it was the political conflict revolving around religious identities rather than denominational difference as such, which made the situation in Ireland so fraught.

Attempts by the British government to use the educational system to indoctrinate Irish children with the ideology of British (or English) nationalism, and rival attempts by many, though by no means all, teachers to capture them for Irish nationalism, formed a backdrop to various controversies that erupted over the teaching of the Irish language, or of Irish history, or indeed of nearly anything that could be forced into rival ideological moulds.

In practice, the conflicts about secondary and university education concerned only small numbers of students until a generation or so ago. Queen's College Cork and Queen's College Galway had at times barely a hundred students on the rolls, even towards the end of the nineteenth century. In 1928–29, UCD had 1,372 registered students, a big increase on earlier years, but still less than 10 per cent of the number today. Even if the Queen's Colleges had not been denounced as 'Godless' by the Catholic bishops, the numbers attending would still have been small. It is easy to forget how few people at advanced level were actually affected directly by the anathemas hurled back and forth between the warring camps on the educational battlefields of the nineteenth century.

Numbers at national schools were a different matter. Although attendance long remained uneven, most parents – even the poorest ones – did try to see that their children got some schooling, as reflected in the decline of the recorded illiteracy rate from 53 per cent in 1841 to 14 per cent by 1901.

The first half of the twentieth century

Although attendance at second and third level did increase gradually in the first half of the twentieth century, it wasn't until the 1960s that the pace of demand began to increase sufficiently quickly to transform education above primary level from a minority interest into a majority concern.

It might seem odd that one had to wait until the 1960s for major changes in educational policy, other than in the Irish language area, given the vigour with which Irish nationalist leaders had denounced the English educational system as a paralysing influence on our national development.

No-one had denounced it more vigorously than Patrick Pearse, whose pamphlet *The Murder Machine*, contains a trenchant assault on the allegedly corrosive influence of the entire education system on the character and intelligence of the Irish people. Pearse sought to elevate education to the highest possible plane. A dedicated teacher himself, a pioneer of bilingual education, with a European perspective, and a concept of multiple intelligence whose full importance has only recently come to be recognised in the most innovatory international thinking, Pearse strove valiantly to raise the level of the potential of education, and of the dignity of the teaching profession. He sought to place the teacher, rather than the administrator, at the centre of the entire system. 'The teachers in fact will be the system', he proclaimed optimistically, as he pronounced teaching to be 'a priest-like ... office', which should offer a vocation to 'the highest souls and noblest intellects of the race'. Nor, however visionary the impulse, did he overlook the fact that if this ideal were to be widely achieved, teaching salaries would have to be high enough to attract the best and the brightest to the profession.

Little of the sort occurred in any planned way. But it is striking how the teacher training colleges and the preparatory schools did produce many teachers of missionary zeal. These colleges offered the main alternative to the civil service for those hoping for a secure and rewarding career but whose parents couldn't afford to send them to university, at a time when very few other jobs were available to the bright children of not only the working class, but the lower middle classes, urban and rural. Many bright children, or their parents, would plot the escape route from the small villages of the west of Ireland, most famously of all from the Dingle Peninsula, to these colleges. Some would naturally forget where they had come from. But many who remembered the obstacles they themselves had to overcome would in turn open doors of opportunity to the bright young children of the next generation who hadn't had the foresight to be born into the lap of luxury. That world, so memorably evoked by the renowned teacher, the late Bryan MacMahon, in his autobiography *The Master*, has now vanished. It is hidden from the youth of today, who almost languidly assume as a right the opportunities that earlier generations of young people had to fight for like starving dogs over a bone. It was a society where many an able child, unless salvaged by priest or teacher, would live out frustrated years knowing they had it in them to have achieved far more with their lives, had they not been trapped by poverty and inequality.

However ungrateful many of today's children are, few would presumably wish to return to the bleak decades. Nor would many want teachers to have to return to the type of working conditions and autocratic regime recorded by Brian MacMahon. In fact, the negotiating skills of teacher trade union leaders of recent years have done the public some service, by securing salary levels for teachers that ensure that the profession continues to attract candidates of high calibre – a prerequisite for good teaching – in a vastly changed world where alternative opportunities threaten to divert talent from the teaching profession.

It wasn't only in their attitude towards teachers that policy-makers in the new independent Ireland paid scant attention to Pearse's injunctions, however much lip service they devoted to his alleged inspiration. The attempt to revive the Irish language by not only making it a compulsory subject, which was perfectly understandable in the struggle for national regeneration, but by teaching primary school children from the earliest years through Irish, reflected little of Pearse's open-minded attitude concerning best practice in bilingual language teaching, which he had closely studied in Belgium.

The teachers found themselves in an impossible position, charged with teaching a language that the wider society, including in large measure the state itself, simply failed to use. What might have been one of the most exciting educational initiatives of the century failed its own terms. It would be left to Israel, in different circumstances, to show how to revive a language. The results of the more recent revisions of approaches to Irish language teaching remain to fully work themselves out. Suffice it to say that the main hope now comes far more from the voluntary commitment behind the Gaelscoileanna, and from Teilifís na Gaeilge, than from earlier approaches.

Education and economic development

It is tempting to attribute the dramatic rise in the numbers going on to second level from under 150,000 in 1955 to nearly 400,000 now, and from 20,000 in third level to more than 100,000 now, to the introduction of free secondary education in Donagh O'Malley's famous coup against the Department of Finance in 1966, and to the subsequent introduction of student grants for third level. These measures did indeed accelerate the growth in numbers, but that growth had already begun, stimulated by the surge in economic growth, which was generating rising incomes and rising expectations.

A relationship between educational investment and economic growth began to be recognised in the 1960s, thanks in part to the report of the OECD committee chaired by Professor Patrick Lynch, which brought an entirely new way, essentially an economist's way, of looking at education. That way can have its own pitfalls, as Professor Lynch himself has warned. But it was badly needed to shake up the rather static mindsets of the time. New types of schools and colleges, from comprehensive and community schools to regional technical colleges (RTCs) and national institutes of higher education (NIHEs), were launched in the 1960s and early 1970s. The feeling grew that, in an age of rapid technological advance, much greater provision needed to be made for technological education.

There had been many earlier calls for a more technically-oriented educational system, not least by Sir Robert Kane, later the first president of Queen's College Cork, in his celebrated work, *The Industrial Resources of Ireland*, published in 1844. Kane's plea for a greater awareness of the importance of technical education for economic development was frequently echoed in the pages of the *Journal of the Statistical and Social Inquiry Society* in subsequent decades. The founding of the Department of Agriculture and Technical Instruction in 1899 marked a modest response to these demands, as did the more ambitious Vocational Education Act of 1930.

The issue is debatable, but it is rather doubtful that the lack of technical education greatly inhibited Irish economic development at the time. There were several more serious obstacles to be overcome. The surge of the 1960s, after all, which is as striking in its own way as the Celtic Tiger phenomenon of recent years, occurred on the basis of the inherited educational system, not of the new one. The RTCs and NIHEs followed, rather than caused, the economic growth of the 1960s.

That is not to say that education was irrelevant to economic development – far from it. The human qualities, however much we tend to dismiss them, taught by home, school and church, inculcated a reasonable level of honesty, reliability, and capacity for co-operation, and helped make Ireland part of the developed, rather than of the underdeveloped, world in terms of human resources and political stability. The more impatient amongst us are prone to point to patent defects in these areas when we contemplate best practice elsewhere. And there are certainly still gaps that can be closed. But it is also right to acknowledge that compared with worse practice elsewhere, there were many positive features of Irish life that offered potential for rapid improvement of economic performance once the political and economic leadership learned how to most effectively mobilise them.

What was true, however, was that the surge of the 1960s could not have been sustained as the world increasingly entered into a knowledge society and an age of information technology, but for the increased investment in technological education.

Third-level expansion

The founding of the two NIHEs in Glasnevin and Limerick, and the launching of the RTC system, brought an unprecedented rate of change to the entire third-level sector. The older universities have also adapted rapidly in many ways, but they might well not have done so but for the bracing winds of competition from the newer institutions.

The RTCs, now rechristened institutes of technology, have been the most rapidly growing sector of all at third level. Their location alone has brought opportunity to a vastly greater number of young people than would otherwise have been the case. Even with the grant system that was introduced in the late 1960s, the cost of third-level education remained prohibitive for most parents. European Union subventions from the Social Fund made a big difference to the cost of going to an RTC. So did the spread of the colleges throughout the country, which reduced the disincentive of distance. The lottery of location, which had discriminated so sharply against families who happened to be in the wrong place, was now rationalised to some extent. Now that the young people of places like Letterkenny, Sligo, Tralee, or Waterford, to say nothing of the NIHE that would become the University of Limerick, could flock to their local institutions, numbers rose rapidly. The instinctive sense of places like Castlebar and Nenagh that a third-level institution makes a huge difference to the viability of a locality is absolutely correct. Every town can't have exactly what it wants, because the country doesn't have the density of population to support expensive institutions everywhere. Nevertheless, 'placeism' remains one of the continuing major areas of discrimination in Irish life, and the location of third-level institutions has been a major influence in lowering that barrier to opportunity throughout the country.

New challenges

Another factor is now growing rapidly in importance. That is age. When educational opportunities were expanding very slowly, people didn't miss out all that much for the rest of their life by being born ten or twenty years too early. That is no longer the case. Huge differences in life opportunities have opened up between, say, eighteen year-olds and thirty year-olds, much less forty or fifty year-olds. Unless there is going to be very sharp discrimination on the basis of age, far more attention must be paid to creating opportunities for adult education for those who want it, or are able to avail of it. Mindsets are still stuck far too much in the rut of age when it comes to thinking about educational opportunity. It is surely myopic to assume that in a rapidly changing world 'education' can end at a young age. It seems inconceivable that one can live a further fifty or sixty years off the camel's hump of so brief and concentrated a period in education. The needs of those who never got the chance to develop their potential in earlier years will differ from those who did. But both need to be thought of as requiring recurring access to education throughout the rest of their lives, on grounds both of equity for the individual and efficiency for the society. The possibility of access, in turn, is rapidly changing, thanks to the potential of technological change for opening up distance education opportunities. It remains to be seen how far the fashionable rhetoric of life-long education will come to be translated into concrete action.

Of the other pressing challenges in education, only three can be glanced at here. It may be true that their school days were the happiest days of their lives for many children. But for many more they weren't. This may have been partly because corporal punishment played so dominant a role in maintaining discipline in many schools until the last generation. But as corporal punishment was also part of the regime for maintaining discipline in many homes, the regime in school probably wasn't all that different from the regime outside it. A more insidious contributor to a child's unhappiness, and one that may have left a more enduring psychological mark, was bullying by other children. A great deal of that may continue today, which can make school life an absolute misery for the victims, who are often the weaker and more sensitive boys and girls. It is particularly difficult to stamp out, and far more attention needs to be paid to it.

What about the plethora of other new demands being placed on teachers in a period of unprecedented change? We may think that Pearse had an exalted view of the role of the teacher. But consider the OECD review of the Irish educational system in 1991, which envisaged the role of the teacher as encompassing 'not only the instructional, the custodial, the inspirational and the disciplinary, but extending to practically all spheres of life, with teachers acting as agents of physical, moral, and spiritual development, emotional and mental health and social welfare'. There would not seem to be much left over after that. Teachers are to be surrogate parents, in effect, to such an extent that one might wonder why parents are needed at all. It may in fact have become high time to begin examining the ideologies underlying OECD and other reports from 'international' organisations; particularly as these reports still tend to be swallowed far too uncritically in Ireland, as if they are invariably the products of detached scholarly, clinical experts rather than possibly at times highly partisan ideological agendas masquerading as 'scientific' documents.

Teachers must now apparently be not only surrogate parents, but surrogate health workers, psychologists, sexologists, and goodness knows what else; and all this at a time when children, increasingly exposed to the oafish values of the tabloid media, seem to many to be displaying an increasing lack of respect for adult authority. One may wonder if the psychological satisfaction derived from teaching has kept pace with the improvement in material circumstances in the light of the changing behaviour patterns diffused by the other great medium of instruction: television.

This is all happening at a time when more and more administrative responsibilities are being piled on teachers. There is nothing in itself wrong with that. On the contrary, there is much to be said for devolving these responsibilities from a highly centralised Department of Education and Science to individual schools and individual teachers, but only on the crucial condition that adequate resources are made available. If that doesn't happen – and it is very rare that it does – the quality of teaching will inevitably suffer. And the quality of teaching is still the single most important influence on the overall quality of the education system.

Education and society

Thirdly, society: what should society – that is to say, we ourselves – expect from education? The Green Paper, the White Paper, and the reports of various conventions, which contain a great deal of valuable reflection, almost invariably stress the importance of educating the whole person. But it is clear that is not what we are actually delivering, at least at third level. It is intriguing to hear Chris Horn, chief executive officer of Iona Technologies, the exciting computer company that began as a Trinity College campus company, lamenting that the engineering degree he did in Trinity, good though it was, 'had no liberal arts module as part of the programme ... I believe that engineering is a creative profession and an exposure to liberal arts is important'.

The compartmentalisation of thinking in higher education means that engineers, with their enormous influence on the way we live, are often educated as if society didn't exist. And engineers are only one example. This principle seems to pervade all higher education. It is arguable that far too much third-level education is tunnel education, producing highly qualified, but sadly narrow, graduates.

If engineers and scientists, and perhaps other professions, learn little about the societies in which they will practice, humanities and social science students, in turn, generally learn little about the implications of scientific and technological change for society, or about the thought processes that lead to scientific discovery. Over a century ago, W.K. Sullivan, the then celebrated president of Queen's College Cork, who was both a chemist and a literary scholar, hoped that it would be one day possible to devise an education that combined the liberal with the technological. It is doubtful that we have made much progress in that direction. The growth of graduate education, which is so important for the future of this country, might seem to offer an opportunity to redress the balance. In reality, it often tends to be even more specialised than undergraduate education.

If we continue in this direction, it could have interesting implications, *inter alia*, for the balance of influence in gender terms in society. Women weren't admitted to university until the late nineteenth century. However discriminatory in principle, this probably made little direct difference in practice, given that only a tiny handful of privileged men got in either. In an age of mass higher education, however, gender differences can have intriguing consequences. There is now a majority of female students in universities, although still a majority of males in the technological institutions. The humanities in particular are now predominantly female.

Given the almost total isolation of science and technology students from social thought, even from social thought concerning the impact of science and technology on society, it is tempting to speculate that the bulk of social, cultural, and even political thinking in coming generations may come to be as dominated by females as it once was by males.

In an age of globalisation, the educational systems of small countries – especially those most exposed to the levelling pressures of mass media – carry an enormous responsibility in helping foster the specific heritage of individual cultures (and the creativity that allows those cultures to continue to make a contribution to the wider world) and avoiding dependence on imported thought. Given that the quality of national performance in a knowledge age will depend overwhelmingly on human factors, and given that the educational system continues to have so crucial a role to play in developing those qualities, our present euphoria about the Celtic Tiger should not blind us, in a moment of hubris, to the scale of the challenge ahead. Only the highest quality of strategic thinking and of management skills, supported by adequate resources, is likely to enable the educational system to respond adequately to that colossal responsibility.

FURTHER READING

There is now a substantial literature on the history of Irish education, although relatively little of it focuses on the relationship between education, economy and society. However, the work of educationalists like John Coolahan and Áine Hyland, and of sociologists like Richard

Breen and Damian Hannan has opened up exciting new possibilities. For a sample of various types of work, see:

Breen, R. (1984), *Education and the Labour Market: Work and Unemployment among recent cohorts of Irish school leavers*, Dublin: Economic and Social Research Institute

Coolahan, J. (1981), *Irish Education: Its History and Structure*, Dublin: Institute of Public Administration

Coolahan, J. (1997), 'Third-level Education in Ireland: Change and Development', in F. Ó Muirchearthaigh (ed.), *Ireland in the Coming Times: Essays to Celebrate T.K. Whitaker's 80 Years*, Dublin: Institute of Public Administration, pp. 191–212

Hannan, D. (1983), *Schooling and Sex Roles, Sex Differences in Subject Provision and Student Choice in Irish Post-Primary Schools*, Dublin: Economic and Social Research Institute

Hyland, Á. (1997), 'Primary and Second-Level Education in the Early Twenty-First Century', in F. Ó Muirchearthaigh (ed.), *Ireland in the Coming Times: Essays to Celebrate T.K. Whitaker's 80 Years*, Dublin: Institute of Public Administration, pp. 166–90

National University of Ireland (1994), *The role of the University in Society*, Dublin

For a case study of the challenge of enhancing access to education in deprived areas, see Catherine Forde, *Making Education work on Cork's North Side: A Strategy Statement* (Northside Education Initiative Cork, 1996)

For an evocation of the realities of national school teaching for much of the twentieth century, see Bryan MacMahon, *The Master* (Dublin, 1992)

The White Paper on Education: *Charting our Education Future* (Department of Education, 1995), reflects the best thinking of the official mind

7

Industrial Development

KIERAN A. KENNEDY

Sir Robert Kane was one of the distinguished supporters of the new Statistical Society founded in Dublin in 1847. Three years earlier he had published his famous book, *The Industrial Resources of Ireland*, in which he surveyed Ireland's capacity for economic development. He concluded that Ireland was well fitted to make industrial progress, and he then asked why Ireland had so far made such little advance. His answer was as follows:

> The fault is not in the country, but in ourselves; the absence of successful enterprize is owing to the fact, that we do not know how to succeed; we do not want activity, we are not deficient in mental power, but we want special industrial knowledge.

The effort to acquire the 'special industrial knowledge' that Kane had in mind has proved to be a protracted struggle, with many ups and downs. This lecture tells the story of that struggle.

The nineteenth century

In the final twenty years of the eighteenth century, a minor industrial revolution had taken place in Ireland. Grattan's parliament encouraged the development of industry: the period was one of general prosperity and many new industries sprang up. The Act of Union of 1801 abolished the Irish parliament and provided for the removal by 1824 of all tariffs on trade between Ireland and Great Britain. The subsequent fate of Irish industry in the nineteenth century gave rise to the nationalist view that Ireland was deprived of a full-blooded industrial revolution by the premature elimination of tariffs – before the indigenous industries were strong enough to withstand foreign competition.

Few historians, however, would accept this interpretation. It failed to take account of the many other influences at work besides the removal of tariffs. Cheaper transport increasingly opened up the Irish market to competition from British goods. The spread of the factory system and the introduction of new machinery spelt doom for many traditional activities anyway, even had tariffs been retained. Ireland lacked significant coal and iron resources, which were closely linked to the new technologies. These technologies led to the concentration of industry in some geographic regions at the expense of others. The declining population after the Great Famine limited the growth of the domestic market in Ireland.

Besides, while the removal of tariff protection was inimical to many industries, it favoured others – in particular the large export-oriented industries, such as Guinness's brewery, which profited from being able to import raw materials duty-free, and to export to larger markets. As a result, manufacturing in Southern Ireland became concentrated in food and drink, which by the 1920s accounted for two-thirds of total manufacturing output.

Free trade also favoured the rise of Belfast as a major industrial city – first through linen and later shipbuilding. Ulster had a considerable linen export industry, even in the eighteenth century, organised on a household basis. The role of Belfast, then a small city of 30,000 people, was that of an organising and trading centre, handling two-thirds of total linen exports. The technology for the power spinning of flax improved greatly in 1825, leading to the demise of rural industry and the concentration of spinning in Belfast. Linen weaving was mechanised in the 1850s and, by reason of its strong competitive position, Belfast linen rapidly captured markets from British linen centres, and Belfast became the chief linen-manufacturing region of the world.

The labour force engaged in the linen mills was predominantly female. The next major industry to develop in Belfast, shipbuilding, offset this gender imbalance. There was already a tradition of shipbuilding in Belfast, the first firm of consequence being that of William Ritchie, who came from Ayrshire in Scotland in 1791. It was, however, the arrival from Tyneside in 1854 of Edward Harland, then aged 23, which gave the decisive impetus to making the Belfast shipyards the largest in the world. Together with his partner, G.W. Wolff, who joined him in the early 1860s, they built the firm of Harland and Wolff, which employed 500 in 1861, and 9,000 by the end of the century.

Other industries grew on the back of these pioneering enterprises, such as the largest rope-works in the UK and a thriving engineering industry to manufacture and repair textile machinery. By the turn of the century the population of Belfast was not far short of Dublin. The contrast with Cork is even more striking: in 1821 the population of Cork was three times that of Belfast, but eighty years later it amounted to only one-fifth. As independence approached, the north-eastern corner of Ireland was the only part that had experienced anything akin to an industrial revolution.

Independence and protection

The partition of the island of Ireland in the early 1920s deprived the new state of the chief centre of industry in the country. The newly independent state was heavily reliant on agriculture, and only one in every twelve workers was employed in manufacturing. Food and drink formed the bulk of exports, and Britain was essentially the only export market.

The policy of most European governments in the 1920s was to get back to the 'normality' that existed before the First World War. From that viewpoint, it is not surprising that a new Irish government avoided any radical departures in policy. But it is strange from the nationalist perspective of Irish economic history. The need for industry, and the use of tariffs to achieve that aim, was prominent in the economic philosophy of nationalist leaders such as Arthur Griffith. Also, the nationalist rhetoric never accepted emigration, and industrial development was the obvious way to provide more jobs at home.

Yet the new Irish government took the view that the prosperity of the economy depended on agriculture. The slogan of the time was 'one more cow, one more sow, one more acre under the plough'. True, some far-sighted steps were taken to develop the infrastructure for industry, such as the Shannon Electricity Scheme, which the artist Sean Keating in his renowned painting, *Night's Candles Are Burnt Out*, depicted as a triumph of the ballot box over the bullet. Much later Keating's son Justin was to become Minister for Industry and Commerce in the 1970s. Back in the 1920s, however, the Cumann na nGael government was reluctant to burden agriculture with higher prices – a likely outcome of industrial protection.

All of this changed radically with the election of de Valera's government in 1932. Indeed pressure for change had mounted even before de Valera took office. By 1931, the worldwide Great Depression, which began two years earlier, had taken its toll on Irish agricultural exports. The tightening of US immigration laws and reduced job opportunities abroad had led to a fall in emigration, so that the need to create jobs at home was still more urgent. The Cumann na nGael government was forced to yield to these pressures by taking power in 1931 to restrict the dumping of cheap imports on the Irish market.

Fianna Fáil was only too happy to use the circumstances of the time to launch its avowedly protectionist policy of industrial development. The objective was partly nationalistic – to keep Irish production in Irish hands – but it also aimed to provide employment and reduce emigration. De Valera was under no illusions that maintaining a larger community in Ireland would involve lower living standards; but he counselled the people 'to forget as far as we can the standards prevalent in countries outside this'.

Widespread use was made of tariffs, quotas, import licences and other such devices to shelter the domestic market from foreign competition. There was also a large extension of state-sponsored bodies in industry and commerce. The 1930s saw the establishment of, among others, Comhlucht Siúicre

Éireann to manufacture sugar from home-grown beet; the Turf Development Board to harvest native peat resources; and the Industrial Credit Company to finance industrial development.

The high levels of protection persisted until the 1960s. This approach led to sizeable increases in manufacturing output and employment in the 1930s, but had little further momentum after the Second World War once the immediate post-war recovery ended. Although manufacturing employment had doubled by then, the initial base was so low that this increase was quite insufficient for Ireland's employment needs, and there was little further progress during the 1950s. The speed and scale of protection had evoked a plethora of undersized firms, often engaged only in the assembly of imported parts of products for sale on the home market. Most of these firms had neither the competence nor the resources to launch into export markets. Foreign enterprise was frowned on but, because of the scarcity of Irish firms with the ability to run large enterprises, many foreign suppliers were allowed to establish plants to preserve their Irish sales. Such foreign subsidiaries, however, were generally prevented by their parent firms from competing in overseas markets.

The chief benefit of protection was that it led to the establishment of many firms that would not have existed without it. Indeed in the troubled world economic conditions of the 1930s it is doubtful if any other approach would have achieved as much. Nevertheless, the hasty and indiscriminate application of the strategy resulted in an industrial base that was weak and vulnerable. There was also no vision about how to progress further once the potential of the small home market was fully exploited.

The outward-looking strategy

The limits of the protectionist strategy became widely recognised in the 1950s, a time when the whole western world was moving to restore free trade. A new outward-looking strategy began to emerge; though it took some time to reach its full flowering. There were three main elements in the new strategy. First, capital grants and tax concessions were provided to encourage export-oriented manufacturing. Second, the

Industrial Development Authority (IDA) was given the task of attracting foreign firms to Ireland, again aimed at exports. And third, protection was gradually dismantled in return for greater access to markets abroad, culminating in an Anglo-Irish Free Trade Area Agreement in 1965 and accession to the European Community in 1973.

Apart from these measures directed specifically at manufacturing, one should not overlook the wider initiatives that later contributed so much to industrial development. Two in particular deserve special mention. First, great efforts were made to improve the physical infrastructure – electricity, telephones, roads and other transport facilities. Second, and perhaps most important of all, was the emphasis placed on education in the seminal report, *Investment in Education*, completed in 1965 under the chairmanship of Professor Patrick Lynch, which foreshadowed the major expansion in education.

The outward-looking strategy worked well in the buoyant world economic conditions prevailing in the 1960s. These were the glory days of Sean Lemass and T.K. Whitaker, still recalled wistfully by older businessmen in the way soccer fans hark back to the era of Jack Charlton and Paul McGrath. The strategy began to be questioned, however, following the first oil crisis in 1973. Although a vast increase in manufactured exports had been accomplished, which has continued up to the present, most of the increase came from new foreign enterprises that exported the bulk of their output.

Concerns about the high and rising dependence on foreign industry were exacerbated in the 1980s, when the flow of foreign enterprise fell, and nearly 10,000 jobs were lost in such firms. This highlighted once more the need for indigenous industry, but the situation of the indigenous firms was even worse. Certainly they had been expected to suffer from the removal of protection, but it was hoped that, aided by the incentive package, many would survive and prosper by taking advantage of export opportunities. In the event, the combined effect of import penetration and the disturbed economic conditions following the oil crises was devastating. After 1966, when the dismantling of protection began in earnest, there was no further rise in indigenous manufacturing employment up to the end of the 1970s, followed by a substantial fall in the 1980s. Between 1980 and 1988, indigenous industry shed more than one-quarter of its workforce. Nor was there much improvement in the share of output exported.

The Telesis Report of 1982, commissioned by the government, documented the fragility of indigenous industry and the excessive dependence on foreign enterprise. It recommended a modification of the outward-looking strategy to give priority to building up a select number of large Irish companies to serve world markets, using sticks as well as carrots for the purpose. The full range of competitive disabilities should be addressed, particularly in marketing and technology, which were previously neglected.

It has to be said that the Telesis prescription was more a signpost to the desired destination than an itinerary of how to get there – so that some time inevitably elapsed before new policies emerged. From the mid-1980s onwards, however, several adjustments were made in industrial policy – directed mainly at stimulating indigenous companies.

These new directions of policy scarcely had time to prove themselves before a further review was initiated, culminating in the Culliton Report published in January 1992. The central message of the Culliton Report was that industrial development strategy goes well beyond industrial policy as traditionally conceived. It called for reform of the tax system, further improvement in the physical infrastructure, and the adaptation of education and training to stress the needs of industry.

The last ten years have seen a dramatic improvement in industrial performance, with total manufacturing employment now 15 per cent higher than in 1987. A big revival in new foreign enterprise has spearheaded the recovery. Foreign firms now account for over three-quarters of total manufacturing exports, and nearly half of total manufacturing employment. Their presence is particularly noticeable in electronics and computing, where many of the world's household names in these activities – IBM, Microsoft, Hewlett Packard and Intel, to name but a few – have major production facilities in Ireland, with rapid further expansion in train; so much so that the educational system is scarcely able to cope with the demand for qualified people.

While foreign enterprises have led the way in the last decade, there has also been a distinct improvement in the performance of native industry, with a rise of 6 per cent in total employment. Particularly encouraging has been the emergence and growth of indigenous electronics firms, specialising in sophisticated niche areas of the market. Native firms as a whole are now exporting more than one-third of their output. As recently as the mid-1980s the bulk of their exports went to only one market: the UK, but now these firms are targeting a much wider range of markets in Europe and beyond. It is too early to say that indigenous industry is firmly established on a new long-term growth path, nevertheless, the success of the last ten years gives solid ground for hope.

Causal factors

To what should we credit the recent industrial transformation? We all know that success has many parents, whereas failure is an orphan – so there is no shortage of claimants of credit for Ireland's industrial 'miracle'. No doubt the fine-tuning of industrial policy following the Telesis and Culliton reports has been helpful. So has the better overall management of the economy, a central feature of which is the national partnership agreements involving trade unions, employers and farmers. Developments in Europe, especially the flow of Structural Funds; the renewed growth of the world economy; and the revival in the stream of foreign enterprise, have all played their part.

It would be unjust, however, not to give credit also to earlier generations which took measures that have now come to fruition. The IDA was far sighted in targeting the high-tech industries at an early date. If Ireland is now on the way to acquiring its own Silicon Valley, this did not happen overnight. Indeed, the groundwork was laid even earlier through the many educational initiatives over the past thirty years, starting with the introduction of free second-level education in 1967. This was followed soon after at third level by the establishment of the first regional technical colleges, now rechristened institutes of technology, of which there are now twelve spread throughout the country, with a new one soon to start in Blanchardstown – a town that is set to become the computer capital of Ireland. From the beginning, the RTCs focused on technician and apprentice education, and have since grown into the largest component of higher education in Ireland. The 1970s saw the establishment of what were later to become new universities – Limerick and DCU – but universities with a difference – dedicated to treating enterprise and the needs of industry as a core part of their educational programmes. One could go back much further to extol the achievements of Kevin Street College, now part of the Dublin Institute of Technology, which pioneered technical education from as early as 1887, with Michael Davitt of Land League fame as one of the ardent promoters.

No-one saw more clearly than Sir Robert Kane the importance of education for industry. In *The Industrial Resources of Ireland*, he put the matter as follows:

> The education necessary for industrial pursuits is very generally underrated in this country, and from this cause alone springs a great deal of our want of industrial knowledge. Our ignorance is so great, that we are even incapable of estimating its extent. If a boy is to be sent to a profession, great care is taken with his education ... But if he is going to trade, education, it is thought, would be thrown away on him.

It would be easy to list many other factors and institutions which could rightly claim a role in Ireland's industrial progress. The really important point, however, is that industrial jobs are now growing rapidly, and doing so at a time when manufacturing employment is falling in most other European countries. To the person searching for a job, this is far more significant than the fact that the volume of manufacturing output in the Republic has trebled in the last twelve years, and is now nearly fifty times higher than it was when the state was founded.

Northern Ireland

The recent industrial progress in the South contrasts sharply with Northern Ireland. It will be recalled that the North was the only part of Ireland to experience an industrial revolution in the nineteenth century. When the country was partitioned, there were more manufacturing workers in the North, even though its population was less than half that of the South. Since then manufacturing employment has fallen substantially in Northern Ireland, and the number employed in the sector is now two and a half times greater in the Republic. What went wrong in the North?

The main reason was the secular decline in the two major industries: linen and shipbuilding, in which the North's initially strong manufacturing base was concentrated. Linen was adversely affected by long-run changes in consumer tastes and habits. Its critical US market was severely damaged by the Great Depression, and the industry never recovered fully again in Northern Ireland.

Shipbuilding was also badly affected by the Great Depression, which led to worldwide overcapacity in shipping, intense competition and weak markets for new ships. A stay of execution was granted to the Belfast shipyards by the Second World War, which brought booming demand for new ships and repair work – a demand that was well maintained in the early post-war years. Subsequently, however, shipbuilding in Northern Ireland shared in the long-term decline of the industry in the UK. Competition from low cost countries and unstable demand were at the root of the decline, but these forces were aided and abetted by poor management, shown by the inability to adapt to changing market conditions and changing techniques of production.

Attempts to provide replacement industries in Northern Ireland enjoyed some success, until the outbreak of conflict in 1969 hampered efforts to attract inward investment. On top of thc unstable political situation came a series of adverse shocks: the two oil crises, the weakening of UK regional policy, and the strengthening of sterling following the exploitation of North Sea oil. Northern Ireland had a catastrophic fall in manufacturing employment up to the mid-1980s, since when the level has been static.

The North is a classic example of an area specialised in a narrow range of activities vulnerable to world market forces. In such a setting, industrial survival depends on adapting to higher value products based on new technologies. Northern Ireland essentially failed to adapt, so that it has suffered massive de-industrialisation. An industrial tradition does not vanish overnight, however, and one may confidently hope that, if stable political conditions assuring permanent peace can be established, the North will in time undergo an industrial regeneration.

Conclusion

In his celebrated statement of the case for industrialisation, written in 1904, Arthur Griffith argued that a country, like a person, needed two arms: industry as well as agriculture. Grafting on Griffith's second arm in the new Irish state has been a long and difficult operation, but at last it is now firmly in place. Yet we must resist the temptation to rest on our laurels. Despite encouraging signs, the indigenous sector of Irish industry has still not fully taken off. Furthermore, as the experience of Northern Ireland shows, even the strongest industrial base can be eroded – unless there is constant renewal of that base. This unceasing process of renewal could do no better than adapt Winston Churchill's dictum to industry: 'the empires of the future are the empires of the mind'.

SELECT LIST OF REFERENCES

Bielenberg, A. (1994), *Industrial Development in Ireland 1780–1907*, Ph.D. thesis, London School of Economics

Girvin, B. (1989), *Between Two Worlds: Politics and Economy in Independent Ireland*, Dublin: Gill and Macmillan

Goldthorpe, J.H. and Whelan, C.T. (eds.) (1992), *The Development of Industrial Society in Ireland*, Oxford: Oxford University Press

Harris, R.I.D., Jefferson, C.W. and Spenser, J.E. (1990), *The Northern Ireland Economy: A Comparative Study in the Economic Development of a Peripheral Region*, London: Longman

Isles, K.S. and Cuthbert, N. (1957), *An Economic Survey of Northern Ireland*, Belfast: HMSO

Kennedy, K.A. (1971), *Productivity and Industrial Growth: The Irish Experience*, Oxford: Clarendon Press

Kennedy, K.A., Giblin, T. and McHugh, D. (1988), *The Economic Development of Ireland in the Twentieth Century*, London: Routledge

Kennedy, L. (1989), *The Modern Industrialisation of Ireland 1940–1988*, Dublin: Economic and Social History Society of Ireland

Kennedy, L. and Ollerenshaw, P. (eds.), (1985), *An Economic History of Ulster 1820–1939*, Manchester: Manchester University Press

McAleese, D. (1971), *Effective Tariffs and the Structure of Industrial Protection in Ireland,* ESRI General Research Series No. 62, Dublin: Economic and Social Research Institute

Meenan, J.F. (1970), *The Irish Economy since 1922*, Liverpool: Liverpool University Press

Ó Gráda, C. (1994), *Ireland 1780–1939: A New Economic History*, Oxford: Oxford University Press

O'Malley, E. (1989), *Industry and Economic Development: The Challenge for the Latecomer*, Dublin: Gill and Macmillan

O'Malley, E. (1998), 'The Revival of Irish Indigenous Industry, 1987–1997', special article in the *ESRI Quarterly Economic Commentary*, April 1998, Dublin: Economic and Social Research Institute

8

Transport

GARRET FITZGERALD

During the first half of the eighteenth century a transport system began to emerge in Ireland which before the end of that century was moving people throughout much of the country on excellent roads. By the early nineteenth century all the main roads radiating from Dublin were served by mail coaches averaging 8 to 9 miles an hour, as well as by the vehicles of several private coaching firms. And after 1815 in the south and west Bianconi's famous cars operated a network of routes, which within two decades were reaching points as remote as Belmullet, Clifden and Cahirciveen.

From the end of the eighteenth century the Grand and Royal Canals also provided services for passengers as well as goods between Dublin and the Shannon – the passenger boats being hauled by galloping horse at speeds of almost 10 miles an hour.

Thus before the age of steam began, Ireland already had a transport system that by the standards of the time was well developed and efficient. Steam was, of course, initially used to power boats and in the 1820s paddle-steamers were operating across the Irish Sea as well as in coastal waters.

The railway system

The railway age began a little later, in Ireland as elsewhere. Ireland's first steam-powered railway – from Dublin to Kingstown, now Dún Laoghaire – was opened in 1834, only three years after the first passenger railway in the world, that from

Liverpool to Manchester. But despite this early start, railways were relatively slow to develop in Ireland. For, despite the fact that by 1845 some 2,200 miles of railways had been built in Britain, only 65 to 70 miles of rail track were then in use in Ireland, on short routes radiating from Dublin, Belfast and Londonderry – to give to the latter city the name it then bore. The very limited scale of this pre-famine Irish rail network reflected a combination of factors: doubts about the commercial viability of railways in the poorer island, policy conflicts at Westminster on the appropriate scale of public finance for Irish railways, as well, probably, as a certain lack of entrepreneurship.

However, in 1846 a standard Irish railway gauge of 5 feet and 3 inches – significantly wider than that laid down for Britain, but the one already in use between Dublin and Drogheda – was finally decided upon, and during the Famine projects for lines to many parts of the country were being promoted and authorised. Their construction was encouraged by the fact that in 1847 the government at Westminster finally decided to supplement private railway capital with public finance, amounting, in today's money terms, to about £50 million.

As a result, in the immediate aftermath of the Famine many lines were built very speedily indeed: within five years more than 700 miles of railway had been opened. My 1853 railway map shows Dublin linked to Waterford, Cork, Killarney, Limerick, Galway and Belfast. Belfast had lines running shorter distances to Armagh, Warrenpoint, Newtonards and Carrickfergus; while a line from Belfast to Derry and onwards to Omagh and to Ballymena was complete except for the section between Ballymena and Coleraine. Ten years later, in 1863, the basic Irish rail network was virtually complete, apart from a couple of outstanding links to towns on the west coast.

But the system thus constructed was highly fragmented and not very profitable. Railways were, of course, very capital intensive, and despite the availability of cheap state capital, fares that were widely regarded as high, and the fact that running costs absorbed only half the revenue, the return on this capital was little more than 3 per cent.

This led to a strong agitation for amalgamation, and indeed nationalisation. A campaign for the latter was in fact launched by the future Lord Ashbourne at a meeting of the Statistical and Social Inquiry Society of Ireland. There followed some consolidation of the system, as a result of which the number of companies had by 1871 been considerably reduced – to twenty-four.

But the total receipts of these twenty-four companies, with their 430 directors, were still no greater than those of a single contemporary Scottish company – a railway that managed to get by with a mere eleven directors. (It was indeed said that at one point if Irish railway company directors had been laid end to end, they would have stretched from Dublin to Cork – an exaggeration of course, but those of 1871 would have stretched for a full half mile!)

However in 1874, after many debates at Westminster, the proposal to nationalise the Irish railways, although having strong support in Ireland, was rejected by parliament; and a later Royal Commission Report recommending amalgamation was also ignored.

Meanwhile passenger canal transport had disappeared in the early 1850s and thereafter road coaches and cars were in the process of being relegated to cross-country routes, or providing services between the main rail lines and the towns in their hinterlands. Between the 1860s and the First World War most of these surviving horse-drawn local services were replaced by branch railway lines.

Many of these branch lines might have been equally well served by rural tramways on the Continental model. This solution was adopted in Ireland only in a few cases in the northern part of the island, for example Warrenpoint to Rostrevor, Victoria Bridge to Castlederg, and Newry to Bessbrook. Many of the branch railway lines were in fact constructed and operated to a higher and much more expensive standard than was justified by the potential traffic, and their construction and operation consequently required local subsidies, known as 'baronial guarantees'. These subsidies were so named because they were provided by the territorial units known as baronies, which before the establishment of county councils were the key units of local administration in Ireland.

The result was that by the time, early this century, when motor transport began to develop as a lower-cost and far more flexible form of short-haul transport, the island of Ireland supported a dense network of railway companies. Eventually there were forty-six different companies operated by twenty-eight different managements, running over 3,500 miles of track. One-eighth of this track consisted of narrow-gauge branch lines.

Many of these lines were natural monopolies – although it may surprise many to learn that immediately before the Great War there were in fact sixteen pairs of points in Ireland between which some kind of alternative services existed – including the sectors from Dublin to Navan, Athlone, Clara, Waterford, and Rosslare and those from Belfast to Derry, Strabane, Cookstown, Antrim and Newcastle.

It should perhaps be added that the services offered were not particularly speedy. Whereas in Britain intense competition in the 1890s led to very fast timings being achieved, which in many cases were not improved upon until the 1960s, the Irish railway system was distinctly sluggish. Thus, apart from the Mail Boat Express, trains to and from Cork immediately before the First World War took, at best, five to five-and-a-half hours to complete the journey – twice as long as is the case today!

By 1913, through underpaying its manual workers – although not its clerical workers – and by charging fares that were generally judged to be high, the Irish railway system overall was earning, in today's money terms, some £125 million profit on £3 billion capital – a return of about 4 per cent.

However, during the Great War the system was taken over by the British government and was badly run down, while the Civil War of 1922–23 saw huge destruction of its infrastructure: a number of companies had to close down their services, and the destruction of bridges, tearing up of track, and derailing of trains interrupted communications on the main lines. A Railway Protection, Maintenance and Repair Corps, comprising unemployed railway workers, had to be established by the provisional government in Autumn 1922 to make temporary repairs and to keep the lines open as far as possible by means of a system of blockhouses and armoured trains.

After the Civil War, the Free State government took over the physical restoration of the system and, having rejected a nationalisation proposal by the Labour Party, decided in 1924 to amalgamate all twenty-six companies that operated exclusively within the territory of the state into a single company: the Great Southern Railway (GSR). However in Northern Ireland and on cross-border routes, the existing companies continued to operate as before.

The challenge of road transport

At that time the character and scale of threat posed by road transport to the largely short-haul Irish railway system was still not fully appreciated. Road passenger and freight services had been slow to develop in Ireland, partly because of the disturbed nature of the country in the years from 1916 onwards, and partly perhaps, because of deficiencies in the road network and a lack of entrepreneurship.

But from the early 1920s onwards road transport began to come into its own, putting both the railways and the city tramway systems under severe pressure. In Ireland, from 1927 onwards, legislation was enacted to protect both the GSR and the Dublin United Tramways Company (DUTC) against competition from motor transport. Laws introduced in the early 1930s gave them compulsory purchase powers over their competitors, which they immediately exercised ruthlessly. By 1935 only a few privately-owned rural bus services survived.

The GSR took a particularly narrow view, restricting the development of the bus network that it had acquired, and failing even to organise feeder services for its rail network. These restrictive measures inevitably failed, and due to competition from private motoring and the growing tendency of firms to use their own vehicles for the transport of their own products, revenue on the extensive rail network fell, and losses were incurred from the 1920s onwards. Even before the Second World War a tribunal of enquiry had to be established to investigate public transport. Its report was inconclusive and it kicked to touch a proposal by the GSR to close down three-eighths of the system.

The deep-seated problem of the railway system was temporarily relieved by the outbreak of the Second World War: a reduction in fuel supplies hit the private transport sector, diverting both passengers and goods to public transport, whose services also had to be sharply curtailed, thus ensuring a very high utilisation of available capacity. The closures of under-utilised lines that had been sought by, but not conceded to, the GSR immediately before the war, were now unavoidable. When the war ended in 1945 many of these branch lines did not re-open. A further drastic paring down of the rail network took place during the following decades, as steam was being replaced by diesel – and in the 1980s by electric power on the Howth-Bray Dublin suburban line.

The DUTC had been established in 1881 to amalgamate and electrify three horse-tram companies that had emerged in Dublin since 1872. In 1896 it took over another company which had just electrified its route to Dalkey and by 1905 it had electrified all its own routes. It eventually operated a network of some thirty tram routes, served by 330 double-deck cars, and in the late 1920s it supplemented these operations with a dozen or more bus routes serving suburbs that its trams did not reach.

During this period many private bus operations sprang up in the city but by 1935 the DUTC had used its compulsory powers to buy out all its competitors, other than the bus services operated by the Great Northern Railway in the north-east quadrant of the city, and the still-surviving St Kevin's bus service to Glendalough. From 1938 the DUTC also started to replace its trams by double-deck buses – hitherto rare birds in Ireland. This process was halted by the onset of the Second World War, but was completed in 1949 – although the Great Northern Railway's Hill of Howth trams survived for another decade.

A significant horse-tramway network had developed in Belfast from 1872 onwards, and was taken over by the corporation in 1904 and electrified almost overnight. Bus competition within the city was eliminated at an early stage by corporation by-laws. However, by 1954 the trams had been phased out and replaced by a combination of motorbuses and, for a period, trolley buses.

The Belfast Corporation by-laws permitted, however, the operation of buses from the city centre to points outside the city boundary. Thus, bus transport was allowed to develop in Northern Ireland in a way that did not happen in the independent Irish state. The contrast between bus service development in the two parts of the island was very marked. Indeed I can recall in 1950 seeing a map of Ireland's bus network prepared by an English geographer, upon which, although the border was not shown, the political division of the island could nevertheless be readily deduced from the totally different density of bus services in its two parts!

Horse trams also operated on a smaller scale in Cork, Galway, and Derry. Those in Cork were converted to electric traction in 1898 and then replaced by buses in 1931, while the Galway and Derry horse trams were replaced by buses in 1919.

Several steam tram companies operated routes out of Dublin and Belfast, the last of which closed in 1933, and Ireland also had a small number of rural tram services of the kind that were very popular in Continental Europe. One of these, the Giant's Causeway and Bushmills tram was, in fact, the first electric tram service in the world, and the horse tram from Fintona Junction to Fintona in Tyrone operated for over a century, from 1854 to 1957.

The fact that Irish public transport, both urban and rural, effectively experienced competition only for a period of about a decade had quite profound effects upon the subsequent structure of transport in Ireland. Given the largely rural character of the Irish economy – as late as 1960 half the population still lived in rural areas or in villages of less than 500 people – it had always been inevitable that private transport would play a disproportionately large role here, absorbing a higher share of resources than in a more urbanised economy at a similar stage of development.

But the early extinction of road competition, and the determination of the railway interest to restrict severely the role of its own road passenger and freight services, had the effect of stimulating even further the growth of private car ownership and of own-account road haulage. While still leaving the privately-owned railway system operating at a heavy loss, this development increased overall transport costs and reduced national competitiveness, thus contributing to the slow growth of the economy between the 1920s and the 1960s.

The establishment of CIE

Between 1945 and 1950 the railway system, with its associated road freight and provincial bus services, together with the Dublin tram and bus system and the moribund canals, had been merged into a single state-owned transport concern: Córas Iompair Éireann or CIE. In 1958 CIE became a national transport monopoly within the state, when the Great Northern Railway, after five years of unsuccessful operation as a company jointly-owned by the governments of the two parts of the island, was split between the two states, the southern part being merged with CIE.

Since then, less than half the costs of a heavily pruned railway system have been covered by revenue. At times governments have seemed content to let the rail system run down, but more recently, with the aid of EU funds, it has been re-equipped and its services have been substantially improved.

In the 1980s the Dublin city bus and provincial bus networks were constituted as separate companies within the CIE group. While both of these have also been subsidised, the scale of subsidisation of the Dublin bus system is low by international standards – undesirably low it could be argued, particularly in view of the level of traffic congestion in a city with a uniquely-constricted centre-city road network. As a result fares are correspondingly high.

The traditional tight restriction on road competition has in recent times been somewhat relaxed, and a serious effort is currently being made to prepare CIE's two road passenger companies to face competition, as required by EU law, and to re-organise the re-equipped railway system to enable it to survive with the lower scale of infrastructural and social aids permitted by the EU.

Sea transport

As an island, Ireland is of course dependent on sea and air services for all its contacts with the rest of the world. The advent of steam in shipping was thus of great importance to our island, which had been at a severe disadvantage so long as it had to depend upon sailing vessels for contact with Britain and the Continent.

As early as 1815 a paddle-steamer was built at Passage West on Cork Harbour, and in 1819 the first cross-channel steamer started to operate from Holyhead to Howth. By 1826 the new City of Dublin Steam Packet Company had fourteen vessels in operation, competing with post office and admiralty steamers on the Dublin-Liverpool route. In the following year Kingstown (later Dún Laoghaire) began to replace Howth as the mail packet port, a process completed within seven years.

For seventy years, from 1850 to 1920, the post office contract was held by the City of Dublin Steam Packet Company. Their fast vessels – which attained world record speeds of 24 knots before the end of the nineteenth century – and those of their successors: the London and North Western Railway (later the London Midland and Scottish or LMS), became familiarly known to everyone in Ireland as the 'mail boats'. Indeed this description survived the post-Second World War transfer of the first-class mail contract to air transport, and disappeared only with the much later advent of car ferries on the Dún Laoghaire-Holyhead route.

For many decades a plethora of steamship services connected the two islands, linking the ports of Cork, Waterford, Rosslare, Dún Laoghaire, Dublin, Greenore, Belfast, Larne and Derry with Fishguard, Bristol, Holyhead, Liverpool, Fleetwood, Heysham, Stranraer, Ardrossan, Greenock and Glasgow. Later the number of routes and services declined and for several decades in the second half of this century there were virtually no daytime services, however, with the introduction of car ferries on a number of routes some thirty years ago, frequencies improved again. Today over one-quarter of a hugely increased volume of traffic between Ireland and Britain still moves by sea.

Ownership of both the British and Irish shipping lines has, however, changed. The bulk of the services are now operated by a Swedish line: Stena, while the Irish-owned services are now operated by Irish Continental Lines. This privately-owned company had begun life as a subsidiary of the now defunct state-owned Irish Shipping Company which had initiated a direct link between Ireland and France in the 1960s.

Despite the fact that the first transatlantic steam-powered crossing was made in 1838 by an Irish-owned vessel: the Sirius, and despite attempts to develop Galway as a terminus for transatlantic steamship services, by 1850 Ireland was effectively out of the transatlantic race. Nevertheless, until the demise of transatlantic passenger steamship services as a result of air competition, Cobh was a frequent stopping point for many transatlantic liners.

Ireland did not succeed in establishing a merchant marine of its own, until forced to do so by the exigencies of the Second World War. Unhappily the state company that was then established: Irish Shipping, foundered forty years later as a result of entering into imprudent long-term charter contracts.

Air transport

As an island Ireland might have been expected to be a natural focus for air transport. Yet after the initiation of civil air transport in 1919, fourteen years were to elapse before the first services to and from Ireland were launched by a Scottish company – a successful route from Glasgow to Belfast, and one from Liverpool to Dublin, that was withdrawn after seven weeks.

In May 1936, Aer Lingus opened the first Irish-owned air services: from Dublin to Bristol (later extended to London), and to the Isle of Man and Liverpool. The outbreak of war led to a temporary cessation of operations, but after some weeks a service was resumed to Liverpool and continued – save for the months immediately before and after D-Day – until the end of the war.

In the immediate post-war years the company over-expanded, opening routes that failed to attract traffic, buying more aircraft than it required and employing an excessive number of staff. However, the cancellation of a premature transatlantic service by a new government in early 1948 saved it from disaster and by 1949 severe retrenchment had put the company on a sound footing. Thereafter it expanded its services steadily and successfully, relaunching the transatlantic service with leased aircraft in 1958 and undertaking this operation with its own aircraft and aircrew three years later.

From 1946 to 1957, 40 per cent of the Aer Lingus shares were owned by state-owned British airlines and the company had a monopoly position on Anglo-Irish routes, but in 1957 this arrangement was terminated and British European Airways joined in cross-channel operations – from which, however, it pulled out again some years later.

From the mid-1980s onwards the liberalisation of air transport by the Irish and British governments has led to intense competition, to which Aer Lingus failed to adjust in the early years of this decade – a situation that required a rescue operation by the government. The result of this competition has been an enormous increase in cross-channel traffic between Ireland and Britain. In the forty years between 1947 and 1987 passenger traffic by sea and air rose from one million to 6.5 million. But in the ten years since 1987 it has jumped to 16.5 million.

The impact of transport improvements

In 1847 a large part of Ireland's external transport capacity was absorbed by hundreds of thousands of emigrants, fleeing the poverty and disease of the Famine years, with no hope of ever seeing their homes or their relatives again. Today the net flow is inbound, not outbound, and almost one-quarter of the journeys between Ireland and other countries – four million journeys in all – will this year have been made by Irish people working abroad returning to see their families here, or by Irish residents visiting relatives working abroad. Efficient, low-cost transport has thus totally transformed the nature of Irish emigration.

That is just one measure of the impact that transport has made upon our way of life during the century and a half of the existence of the Statistical and Social Inquiry Society of Ireland.

9

Money and Banking

ROBERT W. HUTCHINSON

In Ireland the Bible is often misquoted. During this lecture, which traces developments in the banking sector over the last 150 years, bear in mind that money is not an evil in itself. To quote 1st Timothy correctly: 'the love of money is the root of all evil'. Although, from time to time, great passions have emerged in Ireland, none has been for the love of money.

Origins of the modern banking system

At the beginning of the nineteenth century, the Bank of Ireland dominated the Irish financial system by virtue of a royal charter. This charter allowed it to combine some of the functions of a central bank with its commercial banking activities. The rest of the financial system consisted of a number of small private banks. These were narrowly focused on areas of population concentration in Dublin, Cork, Limerick, Clonmel, Waterford and, to a limited extent, Belfast. In the absence of any form of branch banking, the major part of the population, dispersed as it was throughout rural Ireland, had no access to banking facilities.

By the 1830s the structure of the financial sector had been radically altered, particularly over the period 1820 to 1836, when the total number of bank branches had grown rapidly to approximately 130. These branches were operated by a number of joint-stock banking companies, which were formed as a result of legal changes, made in response to the private banking failures of 1820. While most of the joint-stock banks focused on urban centres, concerted and eventually successful efforts were made to extend banking facilities throughout the rural economy. Two banks were founded in 1834 with this specific remit: the Agricultural and Commercial Bank of Ireland, which unfortunately failed in 1840; and the National Bank of Ireland, with Daniel O'Connell as its principal advocate.

The formation of the joint-stock banks created the foundations of the modern financial services industry. By the 1870s this had most, but not all, of the other components that are recognisable today: savings banks, building societies, insurance companies and stock exchanges.

Two factors ensured that the joint-stock banks would continue to dominate financial activity for the rest of the nineteenth century and beyond. First, the opening up of competition under the Banking (Ireland) Act of 1845. This saw the loss of the Bank of Ireland's monopoly banking control in and around the Dublin area. Second, the banking sector's enhanced credibility when it survived the 1857 run on notes and deposits. The result was further growth in the number of bank branches. These peaked at close to 1,300 in the early 1920s; giving Ireland a significantly higher ratio of bank branches per head of the population than Britain and Continental Europe.

By the end of the 1960s, a wave of merger rationalisations, the first for almost one hundred years, saw the disappearance of some of the established names in Irish banking, for example, the Hibernian, Munster and Leinster, Royal, Provincial and Belfast banking companies. Today, the remaining Irish clearing banks still represent the essential core of the financial services industry. The Bank of Ireland and the Allied Irish Banks (the latter incorporating the First Trust Bank in Northern Ireland), are far and away the largest; but the other banks – including the National Irish Bank, the Northern Bank, the TSB Bank and the Ulster Bank – are effective competitors.

Banks and economic development

Analysing the contribution of the banking sector to economic development in Ireland can raise controversial issues. The main criticism, in respect to the nineteenth century, focuses on the extremely slow progress of industrialisation in the major part of the island. This has been explained by arguing that banks were not over-enthusiastic about lending, because they tended to run their loan books below the levels of their deposits. The contradictory evidence, on the successful industrialisation of the north-east of Ireland, has been explained away. The argument is that the Belfast banks were flexible and responsive to the needs of the north east because their senior management was locally based. In contrast, with a number of southern banks having London head offices, a remoteness factor is supposed to have caused a less responsive attitude.

These views can be seriously questioned. First, it was the three Belfast banks that initially engaged in restrictive practices, from as early as 1840. These practices involved agreeing common interest rates and operating in concert, in attempts to hinder other banks from competing in the Belfast banks' geographical markets. Second, there is now a belief that the level of lending by the Irish banks, during the nineteenth century, has been seriously underestimated. Finally, the balance of opinion rests with the view that the South's failure to industrialise lay, not directly with the banks, but in the absence of attractive investment projects. Since Ireland was a fully integrated part of a monetary union, as is explained shortly, the resulting surplus funds were invested at its centre, in London.

Arguably then, nineteenth-century conditions outside of north-east Ireland created an early twentieth-century culture devoid of entrepreneurship. However, the clearing banks could not have been expected to address this problem on their own, especially during the 1920s. Following political independence, safeguarding the stability of the financial system was essential. Imagine what might have happened if either the Irish government or the banks had been profligate with money and a financial crisis had occurred during the Civil War. The innately conservative agricultural economy, whose farmers had valiantly struggled for their land rights and who accounted for a substantial part of Irish bank deposits, would not have tolerated these gains being jeopardised. If such an explosive mixture of events had occurred, Ireland today would probably still be experiencing the aftermath. One does not need to be reminded about the longer run consequences of the 1920s instability in Germany's financial system.

In an environment lacking entrepreneurship, new vehicles were needed to provide more risky and proactive investment banking functions. The first major step in this direction was a public policy initiative in the early 1930s that led to the creation of the Industrial Credit Company, the forerunner of the ICC Bank. One of the other state-sponsored financial institutions, the Agricultural Credit Company, now the ACC Bank, grew out of a need for the state to replace Plunkett's agricultural credit societies, or land banks. These had been formed at the turn of the century but had experienced difficulties in the 1920s due to falling agricultural prices.

The need to ensure that sound money management continued in Ireland was reinforced by the Commission of Inquiry into Banking, Currency and Credit, which reported in 1938. There was concern in the commission over a number of flawed schemes that had been submitted to it. These drew on populist ideas from other countries, aimed at alleviating the Great Depression. The Financial Freedom Federation and Major Douglas's Social Credit Movement suggested ways in which credit could be expanded. The Irish trade union movement advocated taking the commercial banks into public ownership under a single state-banking corporation. Others put forward schemes for funding public expenditure by, for example, repatriating Irish savings invested in London. In response to this, one of the members of the commission, Mr Moynihan, commented:

> It is of vital importance that the people at large should understand that ... to reduce the foreign holdings of a small group of rich men, or those of a considerable number of small investors ... depletes a source of national income, the loss of which would entail general suffering.

But perhaps the best rejoinder to all of these schemes came from Lord Glenavy, who remarked cryptically:

> Anxiety has been shown to the Commission lest the Free State should be open to the charge of failing to keep up

> with the fashions in other countries ... the fashion, however, is designed for those of adequate purse but inadequate personality.

Financing policy

Coming to modern times, with the maturing of its economy, contemporary Ireland has a new competitive ethos that has brought the private-sector clearing and investment banks to the forefront of business financing. These banks, together with those of the state-sponsored financial institutions and the Industrial Development Authority, now adequately meet most of the investment needs of Ireland's industrial and agricultural sectors. Despite this, two financing controversies have arisen. One has an historical ring to it and views the Irish banks as failing to adequately support investment in small businesses. The other concerns a failure to address the funding needs of low-income groups in the personal sector.

Small businesses are heavily reliant on debt financing provided by the banking system. They argue, vociferously at times, that banks place limits on credit availability, charge excessive interest rates, and require business owners to pledge too much of their personal assets, for example their private houses, as security against loan advances.

While few people would go out of their way to express sympathy for their local bank manager, it has to be said that these criticisms are unfounded. Limitations on the size and growth of small firms tend to be self-induced by local business people wanting to keep their firms within the family. They have, therefore, a strong aversion to going public by issuing share capital on the stock exchange. Further, small businesses are inherently more risky than large firms. Naturally enough, this is reflected in the higher interest rates that banks charge and in the personal security they require.

If the Irish financial sector exhibits any failings towards the small business sector, these are to be found in the slow development of venture capital for very high-risk start-up projects.

Turning to low income groups, banks, again, face above average risks in lending to this category. Unlike the small-business sector, however, low-income groups cannot provide personal assets as loan security. To satisfy their borrowing requirements banks would have to meet the whole of the risk involved through very high interest rates. Since this would, in all probability, lead to unwarranted accusations that banks were exploiting the poorest sections of the population, banks have tended to avoid this area of the personal loan market. So, for the first half of the twentieth century, money lenders filled this gap.

By the early 1950s, when the credit union movement was established, this deficiency began to be solved. Since credit unions are community based, they pool local knowledge within each group, or union, reducing risks and enabling funds to be made available to members at very low rates of interest.

The credit union movement has grown substantially throughout Ireland over the last forty years, mainly under the direction of the Irish League of Credit Unions. The movement has now approximately 1.5 million members, covering over 20 per cent of the population, in contrast to about 1 per cent for the equivalent organisations in Britain. The total assets of nearly 600 credit unions are upwards on £1.5 billion, equivalent to roughly one-third of the size of the state-sponsored financial institutions and around one-sixth of the size of the building societies.

Monetary union with Britain

So far, this review of money and banking in Ireland has focused on personal and corporate banking. To gain an overall perspective on the modern financial sector, and its rapid expansion beyond these core activities, it is helpful to return to the beginning of the nineteenth century and to consider how monetary relationships have developed.

At the beginning of the nineteenth century the British and Irish pounds floated freely against gold, allowing the Irish pound to either appreciate or depreciate against sterling. It was sometime after the 1801 Act of Union when the fiscal and monetary relationships between Britain and Ireland were integrated. In 1817 the two exchequers and the public debt were merged; followed by replacement of the floating exchange rate, in 1821, by a fixed exchange rate. The British and Irish pounds were subsequently amalgamated in 1826, creating, to use a phrase which is very topical at the moment, a single currency for Britain and Ireland: sterling. This currency circulated freely throughout the Irish economy until 1927, six years after Irish independence. Even then, the reintroduction of the Irish pound – under the guidance of the Currency Commission, the forerunner of the Central Bank of Ireland – did not alter the essence of the monetary union with Britain. This remained in place until 1979 when, at the Irish government's instigation, Ireland introduced capital controls and entered the European Exchange Rate Mechanism. With sterling remaining outside, the one to one parity relationship with the Irish pound was broken.

Incidentally, the poet Yeats chaired the committee that was charged with designing the new coins introduced in 1928. The Irish pound was originally referred to as the Saorstát pound, with the term 'Saorstát Éireann' appearing on the coinage. This was replaced by 'Éire' in 1939.

In a monetary union, both the personal and banking sectors in a regional economy exhibit a preference for investing outside their region in the monetary union's central financial markets. As already indicated, in Ireland's experience, this was the case. As the British economy grew rapidly in the second half of the last century, Ireland accumulated liquid assets and British government securities in London. Even in the 1950s, as much as half of the savings held with the Irish banks were invested there.

Dublin as a financial centre

The reversal of this situation commenced with the establishment of the Central Bank of Ireland in 1943, but did not really begin in earnest until the latter part of the 1960s. Then, the main clearing banks transferred the remaining part of their external reserves to the Central Bank of Ireland, in Dublin, and measures were introduced to improve the saleability of Irish government bonds or gilts. In addition, with a number of foreign banks setting up branches in Ireland, to service the growing number of multinational companies which were creating inward investment, the environment was set for the growth of Dublin as a financial centre.

In the intervening years, an influential report *The Control of Banking*, commissioned by the Irish Banks Standing Committee, and further structural changes, helped to create today's vibrant and broadly-based financial services sector. Apart from entry into the European Monetary System, the other changes included:

- the abolition of the interest rate cartel, which existed from the early part of this century;
- the removal of capital controls, under the European Union's single market programme;
- the breaking down of barriers between the traditional banking, building society and insurance markets; and
- the dramatic growth of the Irish economy over the last ten years.

Currently, therefore, Dublin contains not only thriving money and capital markets, which trade in shares and government bonds; but also an important foreign exchange market, with a daily turnover equivalent to between one and one and a half billion Irish pounds. In terms of its range of financial services, Dublin can now be placed ahead of Edinburgh which, outside of London, has been traditionally viewed as the most important financial centre in Britain and Ireland. By contrast, Belfast is essentially a regional banking centre.

The international dimension achieved by Dublin has been further enhanced by the creation, in the late 1980s, of the International Financial Services Centre (IFSC). The IFSC concentrates on fund management and related activities and, through its tax incentives, has attracted prominent European, American and Asian financial institutions. There are over 350 projects in the IFSC, accounting for around 2,000 jobs.

The rapid rise in living standards in the second half of the twentieth century has seen an expansion of building society activity to meet the growing aspirations for home ownership. Also, there has been a very significant increase in the size of the insurance sector and in pension fund management, reflecting the high proportion of young people in the workforce.

Overall, with around 40,000 employees in financial services as a whole, Ireland has developed a breadth and depth to this sector of its economy which could not have been envisaged in 1979, when the Irish government terminated its 150-year monetary union with Britain.

Monetary union with Europe

What of the future? Ireland is committed to participating in another monetary union, Europe's single currency, from its projected start date on 1 January 1999. Will the recent developments in the Irish financial services sector be further enhanced, or reversed, in the opening decade of the new millennium?

While the Irish economy as a whole might benefit if European monetary union takes place, its financial services sector will, at least in the medium term, contract somewhat. As explained, there is a tendency in a monetary union for money and capital markets to concentrate in one or two geographical centres, probably London and Frankfurt in this case. Further, with the likely emergence of Europe-wide financial assets, trade in some of the assets on the Dublin financial markets may shrink.

The Central Bank of Ireland will lose a number of its functions to the European Central Bank. In the case of the clearing banks, significant income losses from foreign exchange dealings are anticipated, since the currencies of countries, which participate in European monetary union, will disappear. Given that the clearing banks have a key role to play in introducing the single currency, or euro, to the rest of the Irish economy, they will face sizeable, but short-term, currency changeover costs.

On a more positive note, the euro is likely to increase the investment opportunities open to the Irish pension-fund industry due to the removal of exchange rate risk across countries participating in the single currency.

European monetary union, if it takes place, is the final step in the completion of the single market in financial services, which was introduced at the end of 1992. In that sense, the single currency may simply accelerate the pan-European competition in banking, which this programme has already initiated. The single currency may, however, encourage predatory takeover activity and could, conceivably, result in the demise of some Irish financial institutions, at least in terms of domestic ownership stakes. As Maurice O'Connell, the Governor of the Central Bank of Ireland has argued in a recent address to the European Finance Convention:

> The single currency will change the financial environment and it is reasonable to be concerned that there may be some competitive advantages for larger [European] institutions big enough to exploit pan-European markets.

In the longer term, a freeing up of cross-border trade and a common, anti-inflationary, monetary policy might raise growth rates in the European economies. Eventually, therefore, if there is increased investment and personal income growth in Ireland, its financial services sector could recoup its short to medium-term loss of business and indeed expand with the rest of the economy.

There is some concern, however, over Britain's opt-out position. While Ireland has made enormous strides in building its trading relationships with Continental Europe and the rest of the world, Britain remains an important export market, especially for indigenous industry. If Britain does not adopt the single currency then adverse exchange rate movements between sterling and the euro could have a negative impact, particularly on the small business sector.

There is a sharp contrast between the process of integration that occurred in Ireland's and Britain's cases at the beginning of the nineteenth century, and the potential completion of European integration in the early years of the twenty-first century. Political union in 1801, was followed by fiscal integration in 1817, and finally monetary union in 1826. For ardent Europeans, the order of European integration is reversed: monetary union precedes fiscal harmonisation and the eventual goal of a federal Europe. In European money and banking terms, this reverse order might prove to be relatively unstable.

Certainly in the nineteenth century, various European programmes aimed at monetary union were short-lived, for example the Latin Monetary Union formed in 1865 between France, Belgium, Switzerland and Italy. Without political union, the claim, under the present day single currency proposals, that exchange rates will be irrevocably fixed from 1 January 1999, is misleading. These exchange rates may be viewed by international financial markets as unsustainable. This scenario is most likely if different economic policies, across the countries which adopt the euro, lead their representatives within the European Central Bank to pursue national interests, and produce a weak, inflation-prone monetary policy.

Political union between Britain and Ireland gave sufficient time for these two countries to prepare for their monetary union; and sustained it. While the link with sterling was maintained for a long period following Irish independence, it was nevertheless eventually broken.

Conclusion

In conclusion, if there is a love of money in the banking community it is counterbalanced by a desire for stability. Despite the struggles and difficulties in Ireland over the last 150 years, the Irish banks have continued to exercise prudence in money management. This contribution to political stability has never been fully recognised.

Participation in the single currency, if it goes ahead, is a momentous step. Whatever the outcome, and it is not completely clear that it will be to the net benefit of the economy; bankers, at least in Ireland, can be expected to provide the skills appropriate to whatever new monetary regime emerges.

FURTHER READING

Commission of Inquiry into Banking, Currency and Credit (1938), Dublin: Stationery Office

Davy, Kelleher, McCarthy Economic Consultants (1984), *The Control of Banking in the Republic of Ireland*, Dublin: Davy, Kelleher, McCarthy

Hutchinson, R.W. (1996), 'Economic Implications for Ireland of EMU: The Financial Services Sector', in T. Baker, J. Fitzgerald and P. Honohan (eds.), *Economic Implications for Ireland of EMU*, ESRI Policy Research Series Paper No. 28, Dublin: Economic and Social Research Institute

McGowan, P. (1990), *Money and Banking in Ireland: Origins, Development and Future*, Dublin: Institute of Public Administration

Ollerenshaw, P. (1987), *Banking in Nineteenth Century Ireland*, Manchester: Manchester University Press

O'Connell, M. (1997), 'EMU and Irish Monetary Policy', *Central Bank of Ireland Quarterly Bulletin*, Spring, Dublin

10

Changing Work Patterns

BRENDAN J. WHELAN

According to Sigmund Freud, all that matters in life is love and work. Over the centuries, love has always been regarded as a good thing, but work has been viewed variously as a divine blessing and a grim necessity. The medieval monks believed that *laborare est orare* (to work is to pray). On the other hand, Oscar Wilde described work as the 'curse of the drinking classes'. Our task here is to examine how the nature of work in Ireland has changed over the past century and a half. We will see that all aspects of working life have been fundamentally transformed: who works, and who doesn't; what people work at; how long they work each day; at what age they start to work and at what age they cease. All have changed utterly.

The main force driving these changes is what Adam Smith called 'the division of labour'. The relentless process of economic development is based on increasing specialisation and technological advance, which permit goods and services to be provided ever more cheaply and more efficiently. Think of the cost and labour required in the Middle Ages to produce, say, a knife. Today a plastic knife can be mass-produced at so low a cost as to be used once and then disposed of. The alliance of the division of labour with a competitive market leads to a dizzying cycle of growth and decline. New processes demanding new skills are tried. They fail. They are tried again. They succeed. Occupations once highly valued become redundant. Where nowadays would a cooper find employment? Yet this was once a common and very skilled trade. Firms are set up to exploit new opportunities and they grow with staggering speed.

'Microsoft' is today a household name and one of the most powerful companies in the world. But thirty years ago the company, its products and the types of job it generates were all unheard of.

Occupations and industries

Let us begin by looking at the occupations and industries in which Irish people have worked during the past 150 years. In the Ireland of the 1840s, over half of the working population relied on agriculture, much of it of a very primitive kind providing bare subsistence from tiny holdings. While the population fell throughout the following eighty years, the proportion of the labour force engaged in agriculture remained roughly constant at about 50 per cent. From the late 1920s there began an inexorable decline in the proportion engaged in agriculture, so that today just under 10 per cent of the employed labour force works in the broad agricultural sector comprising farming, forestry and fishing. The rate of decline has been particularly marked since 1960.

During the nineteenth and early twentieth century, Ireland failed to industrialise to the same extent as other European countries, which meant that the proportion of workers engaged in industry and services remained roughly constant with about one-fifth of the labour force working in industry, while one-third had service occupations. Since 1926, the proportion in industry has risen slightly, so that today it accounts for one worker in four. At the same time, the proportion engaged in services has grown massively. Today, of all those who are engaged in paid work, about three in every five are engaged in service occupations.

One of the most striking features of the transformation that has taken place is the movement of production out of the household and into separate settings, such as factories and offices. Like farmers, most of the numerous textile workers in the early nineteenth century worked in their homes. By 1900, their numbers had shrunk to one-eighth of their previous level and most of those remaining now worked in factories and linen mills.

The irresistible force of the division of labour also brought huge changes to the nature of agricultural work. Farms became more mechanised and specialised. Even as recently as thirty years ago, many farmers still had vegetable gardens, reared chickens, killed the occasional pig or lamb for their own consumption, and drank their own milk. Today, farmers, like the rest of us, buy most of their food in the supermarket. There has been a particularly sharp decline in the numbers of agricultural labourers and of family members classified as 'assisting relatives' on farms.

The enormous expansion in 'services' includes work in sales and commerce, such as shop assistants and insurance agents; those employed in transport and communications, such as drivers and delivery staff; professionals, such as doctors and accountants; and the various kinds of public servants and administrators. Today, the fastest growing occupations in Ireland's expanding labour force include business and legal professionals, computer specialists and managers. Forecasters expect the strong growth in service activities to continue.

Employment and gender

We tend to think that a high level of participation by women in the labour force is a modern phenomenon. This is not the case. In the late nineteenth century, about one-third of all those classified as being at work were female, and were mainly engaged in making textiles in the home and as domestic servants. The female share of the labour force fell to one-fifth in the early 1900s, and remained below 30 per cent until the 1980s, before rising to today's level of 37 per cent.

These figures are, however, controversial, because there is a sharp dispute over how women's work in the home should be classified. Statisticians define work as any activity which involves payment, or which is directed to the production of *goods* for direct consumption by the household. However, this definition excludes any *services* that are both produced and consumed within the household, such as cleaning or cooking. This leads to the anomaly that if a man marries his housekeeper, the measured level of economic activity falls, even though the woman in question may continue to perform an identical range of domestic tasks. It is not surprising, then, that feminist commentators sometimes refer to history as 'his story'. Work done by women has tended to be under-reported and this contributes to making females invisible in the historical narrative. Some sociologists, by using a more inclusive definition of work, have shown that work by women is greater in volume and more stable over time than the conventional figures suggest (Fahey, 1992).

Possibly the most interesting feature of female employment patterns over the last century or so is the fact that 'domestic service' has practically disappeared. In 1881, over half of all working women were classified as domestic servants. Today, only 4 per cent remain. How can this amazing drop be explained? One factor is certainly the lower productivity in domestic services compared with other parts of the economy. As economic development proceeds, opportunities open up in factories and in new forms of commercial work, all offering higher wages. This makes domestic service less attractive to new recruits. At the same time, the toil involved in housework has been much reduced by such inventions as fridges, washing machines, central heating and vacuum cleaners. Nor must it be forgotten that the working conditions for domestics in nineteenth-century Ireland were very harsh. As one of Shaw's characters remarks ironically, 'when domestic servants are treated like human beings, it is not worthwhile to keep them'.

Working time

Working time has also changed dramatically since the 1840s: the normal working day has shortened, and so has the usual number of days worked per week. The introduction and extension of paid holidays has reduced the working year. At the start of our period, daily working hours and annual working days were both very high. Fifteen or sixteen hour days were common. Indeed, since the majority of workers at the time were self-employed farmers, the very concept of 'usual working hours' would not have been very meaningful for them. The farmer's hours are dictated by the pressures of climate, season and daylight. By contrast, the employee's contract of employment is based on supplying a specific number of hours for a certain wage. Thus, working hours have always been a key feature of the wage bargain. A joker once said that even when the bees went on strike it was for ‘shorter flowers and more honey’.

Scholars (Hinrichs, 1991) have noted the changing preoccupations of employees and their unions about working hours. In the early stages of industrialisation, the prime concern was to allow workers enough time to recuperate from the stresses of work. In the 1950s and 1960s, the idea of a right to a certain amount of leisure came to the fore, and negotiations on working time were directed at improving employees’ overall quality of life. Since the 1970s, there has been increased concern with flexibility, that is, with tailoring working time to fit in with more varied and individualised lifestyles. Flexi-time, job-sharing and increased part-time working are all ways in which workers have tried to juggle competing demands, such as family, leisure and study. Employers have facilitated this move away from standardised hours because it improved their ability to respond efficiently to customers’ demands.

In Ireland during this century, there have been three distinct phases or ‘rounds’ during which working hours were reduced. The first occurred just after the First World War and secured a reduction of the working week to 48 hours for many groups of workers. This round was mainly precipitated by fears of unemployment and a desire to share the available employment more equitably.

From the 1930s up to the 1960s, a six-day 48-hour week remained the norm. The second round of reductions began in 1959, when the newly united Irish Congress of Trade Unions adopted the 40-hour working week as a policy objective. This was gradually achieved over the next ten years and the 40-hour week was consolidated by the various national wage agreements of the 1970s. The third round of reductions occurred as a result of the Programme for National Recovery negotiated in 1987, which resulted in a 39-hour standard working week for most manual workers.

Of course, the standard working week is far from universal. Part-time work has increased markedly in recent years. In 1993 it accounted for about 5 per cent of total employment. Today this proportion has more than doubled to 12 per cent. Part-time employment is much more common among women than among men and is heavily concentrated in service sectors, such as distribution and catering. On the other hand, many people work overtime, either paid or unpaid, regularly or occasionally. Survey data (Fynes et al., 1996) suggest that managerial and professional workers report somewhat longer working hours and higher levels of unpaid overtime than other categories of employee. Self-employed people like farmers and shopkeepers report longer working hours than any other category.

Work across the life cycle

Not only has the number of working hours changed, so also have the ages at which people commence employment, and when they cease working. In the nineteenth century, most people had left school by the age of 12. Indeed starting work in one's very early teens was still common until the 1960s. For instance, in 1961 two-thirds of those aged 14 to 24 were at work or seeking work. Today, this proportion has fallen to less than 40 per cent. The reason for this big fall is, of course, the vast expansion in educational participation. Nowadays, about half of all those leaving second-level education each year go on to some form of third-level study. This rapid growth is driven by the demands of the economy for an ever-increasing range of skills and competencies.

Governments nowadays invest huge sums in training and education and countries vie with each other to achieve the best-educated labour force. Economic research suggests that these policies, which have been pursued consistently by successive Irish governments, played a major role in our current economic success (Duffy et al., 1997). Much effort is devoted both by government agencies and by the educational institutions themselves to designing courses relevant to the emerging needs of industry. It will always be a difficult task for educational policy to manage the tension between the short-run demands for relevance and the longer-term need to lay solid foundations for future learning.

Working lives have also become shorter because of earlier retirement. The very idea of 'retirement' is essentially a modern invention. In nineteenth-century Ireland most people ceased work gradually, usually as their health deteriorated. When they were no longer able to work, they were cared for by their families. This pattern of gradual retirement was especially prevalent among farmers and the self-employed and persists to some extent up to the present day. Because they continued at work, the elderly were slow to hand over the running of the farm or business to their heirs. Retaining control meant that the family would respect and care for them. The social consequences of late inheritance have been much discussed, and psychologists have emphasised the frustration and loneliness imposed on ageing single children waiting to inherit. The attempted patricide in *The Playboy of the Western World* is an extreme manifestation of such negative feelings.

In the twentieth century, the quickening pace of economic change meant that employers had an increasing need to dispense with older workers, but also to provide for them. This was achieved by extending more widely the right to a pension, a benefit that was originally the exclusive preserve of certain public sector occupations, such as soldiers and civil servants. The state also started to play an increasing role in the provision of pensions. In 1908, the UK parliament passed the Old Age Pension Act, which provided a limited means-tested payment to those over seventy. As in other countries, these payments were originally seen as 'social assistance for the indigent, not a retirement wage for a population of superannuated elders' (Myles, 1984). The idea of a universal right to social security in old age only became widespread in the boom following World War II. In Ireland, this took the form of the contributory social insurance scheme introduced in 1961 and extended to all employees in 1974.

The introduction and extension of pensions, often with a compulsory retirement age, has had a striking effect on the numbers of older people in employment. In 1926, three-quarters of all men and one-quarter of women aged 65 and over were still working. Today less than one man in seven works past the age of 65, and less than 3 per cent of women.

Combined with rising life expectancy, this has meant a huge increase in the retired population, or those of the 'third age', as it is sometimes called. These people are healthy, active and well-educated and their numbers are increasing. Budding social engineers could usefully try to devise schemes to harness the talents and experience of the active elderly.

Unemployment

Denial of the opportunity to work has long been regarded as one of the great social evils, leading to poverty and all its attendant miseries, such as malnutrition, crime and social degradation. Even today, when social welfare provision is reasonably well developed, social surveys suggest that 'unemployment' is still regarded as the single greatest problem facing the country. In the nineteenth century, the only options open to those without work were the grim regime of the workhouse or the emigrant ship. In 1911, a limited scheme of social insurance against illness and unemployment was introduced for certain manual employees. This was based on contributions from the workers themselves, their employers and the state, with the benefits being confined to those who had made contributions. Those not covered by the scheme still had to rely on the inhumane and oppressive Poor Law system. One of the earliest acts of the new Irish government in the 1920s was to amend this system by abolishing the workhouses as institutions. From then on, assistance to those in need was to be provided entirely by means of 'Outdoor Relief' which was renamed Home Assistance. However, the basic system, including the criteria for whether relief could be granted, remained fundamentally unchanged.

In 1933, the Fianna Fáil government introduced a means-tested unemployment assistance scheme financed from general taxation. Since then, the range and quality of unemployment schemes have been substantially improved. Coverage of the social insurance system was extended to all employees in 1974 and the rates of benefit have risen continuously in real terms. Today, the safety net provided by the social welfare system ensures a basic standard of living for all the unemployed. The adequacy of the payments may still leave something to be desired (see Callan, Nolan and Whelan, 1996) but, considered in the long term, a truly remarkable improvement in the living standards of the unemployed has been achieved in the past century.

The level of unemployment is often used as an indicator of how well the economy is performing. The census of population suggests that from the 1920s until the late 1970s the level of unemployment averaged about one person in twenty in the labour force. This proportion rose and fell from year to year in response to fluctuations in both the Irish and British economies.

In the late 1970s, all European countries experienced a massive rise in unemployment, caused by the sudden increase in oil prices and the slowness of western economies to adapt to it. Ireland suffered more severely than most. From a level of one in twenty in the early 1970s, unemployment rose continuously until by the mid-1980s almost one person in five was unemployed. In the late 1980s, the prospects for the Irish economy were bleak: unemployment was at an unprecedented level and the state of the government finances was a cause for serious concern. At this point, strong action, in the form of budget cuts and expenditure restrictions, was taken by the government, spearheaded by the then Minister for Finance, Ray MacSharry. These steps, combined with an improving international environment, changes in the structure of the labour force and the level of education, and with increased transfers from the European Union, brought about a major transformation. Today, unemployment has shrunk to about 10 per cent of the labour force and the economy seems set on a path of balanced and sustainable growth. The unemployment rate is likely to go on falling over the next ten years. From being an economic laggard all its life, Ireland has recently been described by *The Economist* magazine as 'Europe's shining light'. Foreign experts who once studied the Irish case for its eccentricity and poor performance, now try to analyse the conception and birth of the 'Celtic Tiger'.

Unemployment is, however, still a serious problem, even though now more tractable than for many years. Not having a job, or living in a jobless household, is one of the factors most closely related to poverty (Callan et al., 1996b). Unemployment is heavily concentrated in certain groups within the population: the poorly educated, those with low skills and those with a history of low status jobs. Even when unemployment was at its peak, three in every four adults had never experienced unemployment at any time during their careers (Callan et al., 1989). A minority of people live constantly with unemployment and the fear of unemployment: for the majority it is something they hear about but never experience.

Another striking feature of unemployment is how it is passed on from one generation to another. In spite of the massive growth in educational opportunities, over 30 per cent of school leavers with unemployed fathers are themselves without a job a year after leaving school, compared with less than 5 per cent of children with parents in professional occupations (McCoy and Whelan, 1996). It is often assumed that unemployment is concentrated exclusively in black spots in urban areas. This is not the case. Unemployment is geographically pervasive, and rural counties like Donegal and Wexford have unemployment rates that are among the highest in the country. Unemployment in Ireland is also remarkable for its long-term nature. Two-thirds of the Irish unemployed have been without work for more than a year, a figure that is among the highest in the European Union.

Coping with the problem of unemployment must be at the top of the political agenda. Clearly, training and reintegration measures have a key role to play. So also has increased focus on preventing pupils from leaving school early. A significant minority still leave the educational system with poor qualifications, or none at all, and they face insuperable difficulties in the labour market. It is also vital to improve the process of matching jobs and applicants. Finally, the tax and welfare systems need to be kept under continuous review to maintain the incentive to work.

Conclusion

There is no doubt that working patterns will continue to evolve in the future, often in ways we cannot now foresee. We may yet become the dreary automatons envisaged by Orwell in his book, *1984*. More optimistically, it may be possible to approach the ideal society proposed by Karl Marx and Frederick Engels:

> Where nobody has one exclusive sphere of activity but each can become accomplished in any branch he wishes, (making it possible) to do one thing today and another tomorrow, to hunt in the morning, fish in the afternoon, rear cattle in the evening, criticise after dinner, just as I have a mind, without ever becoming hunter, fisherman, herdsman or critic.

REFERENCES

Callan, T., Nolan, B., Whelan, B.J. and Hannan, D.F. with S. Creighton (1989), *Poverty, Income and Welfare in Ireland*, General Research Series No. 146, Dublin: Economic and Social Research Institute

Callan, T., Nolan, B. and Whelan, C.T. (1996a), *A Review of the Commission on Social Welfare's Minimum Adequate Income*, Policy Research Series No. 29, Dublin: Economic and Social Research Institute

Callan, T., Nolan, B., Whelan, J., Whelan, C.T. and Williams, J. (1996b), *Poverty in the 1990s: Evidence from the 1994 Living in Ireland Survey*, Dublin: Oak Tree Press

Duffy, D., Fitz Gerald, J., Kearney, I. and Shortall, F. (1997), *Medium-Term Review: 1997–2003*, Dublin: Economic and Social Research Institute

Fahey, T. (1992), 'Housework, the household economy and economic development in Ireland since the 1920s', *Journal of Sociology*, vol. 2, pp. 42–69

Fynes, B., Morrissey, T., Roche, W.K., Whelan, B.J. and Williams, J. (1996), *Flexible Working Lives: The Changing Nature of Working Time Arrangements in Ireland*, Dublin: Oak Tree Press

Hinrichs, K. (1991) 'Working-time development in West Germany: Departure to a new stage' in K. Hinrichs, W. K. Roche and C. Sirianni (eds.) *Working Time in Transition – The Political Economy of Working Hours in Industrial Nations*, Philadelphia: Temple University Press

McCoy, S. and Whelan, B.J. (1996), *The Economic Status of School Leavers 1993–1995: Results of the School Leavers' Surveys*, Dublin: Department of Enterprise and Employment and the Economic and Social Research Institute

Myles, J. (1984), *Old Age in the Welfare State: The Political Economy of Public Pensions*, Boston: Little Brown

Ó Gráda, C. (1994), *Ireland: A New Economic History 1780–1939*, Oxford: Clarendon Press

11

Family Life

FINOLA KENNEDY

Three chapters

Writing in the middle of the last century, John Mitchel remarked, 'Land in Ireland is life'. Mitchel's observation provides a key to understanding the family life of the majority of people then, and for much of the time since then. Access to land was the crucial factor facilitating marriage and family formation until well into the twentieth century. The story of family life in Ireland during the 150 years since Mitchel wrote, and since the Statistical Society was founded, falls into three chapters.

The years from the Famine until the first decade of the twentieth century comprise the first chapter. Two Acts of Parliament passed in the early years of the century were critical to family life. These were the Wyndham Land Act in 1903, which marked the end of the land struggle and paved the way for tenant ownership; and the Old Age Pension Act in 1908, which reduced the economic dependence of old people on their children. The years from the Wyndham Act to 1959 comprise the second chapter. These years may be described loosely as that of 'de Valera's Ireland', when the family homestead was idealised and the roles of men and women were segregated. In 1903 de Valera was a 21-year-old teacher; in 1959, he left active politics. The chapter unfolding since 1960 recounts the modernisation of the family and of Irish society.

The predominant feature of the first phase was the farm family; in the second phase the farm family was joined, in growing numbers, by the urban family, generally dependent on a male breadwinner; while in the third phase, a variety of family forms has emerged that increasingly includes partnerships formed without marriage, or re-formed consequent to the break up of marriage.

The phase following the Famine until early in the twentieth century was characterised by a move towards delayed marriage with a high proportion of the population remaining unmarried. The *General Report* of the 1871 Census explains the low marriage rate in terms of a lack of material development, saying, 'The Irish beyond all dispute are a nation whose individuals will marry when they can, and be celibates only when they must' (p. 54). The fertility of those who married in the post-famine era remained high. The fertility of marriage was investigated in the all-Ireland censuses of 1841 and 1911. The most remarkable finding was 'the constancy of the rates over so extended a period' (Geary, 1935/36).

As the twentieth century opened there were many signs of rising living standards. The shipyards in Cork and Belfast were flourishing, along with brewing, distilling, mineral waters and biscuits, the linen industry was prospering in the North and woollens and hosiery were developing in the South. The so-called 'working classes' were emerging and the 'breadwinner father' taking his place alongside the family homestead as the source of family livelihood. While marriage rates remained extremely low in rural areas, they were higher in urban areas; a fact concealed in the total marriage rate. Most significantly a long-run decline in the fertility of marriage set in; the decline since the 1911 Census has been more or less uninterrupted.

The 1903 Land Act provided security and improved economic opportunities for the farming community, while poorer areas benefited from the introduction of the Old Age Pension in 1908. This relative prosperity had social effects: Ireland might have been feudal in the 1870s as George Moore remarked, but thirty years later something resembling a middle class had emerged (Meenan, 1970, p. 16). In some areas atrocious poverty persisted. Eighty years after the Famine, death from starvation still occurred. In 1927 a mother and two children died from starvation in the Beara Peninsula in Cork, a tragedy immortalised in a novel by Peadar O'Donnell (Fanning, 1983).

Gradually, economic and social changes undermined the viability of the small family farm. Included among these was a critical change in the relationship between the farmer and the farm worker subsequent to legislation on pay and hours of work in the late 1930s. As a result of this many farmers claimed that they could not afford to hire workers. Some became even more dependent on family labour. Small family farms were maintained intact through a combination of high celibacy rates, high emigration rates and high, though now slowly declining, fertility, amongst those who did marry, thus ensuring a pool of family labour to work on the farm. The demise of the small family farm, which was finally marked by the transformation of Irish agriculture following entry into the EEC in 1973, was the catalyst leading to the modernisation of family patterns since the 1960s.

In the past four decades, and in particular since 1980, family life in Ireland has been transformed. During the past fifteen years marriage has been losing popularity; the age at marriage has risen sharply, while the risk of marriage breakdown has increased. (Kennedy and McCormack, 1997). At the present moment close to 100,000 persons in the state have experienced marital breakdown (Census 1996, vol. 2). Births, which rose to a twentieth-century peak in 1980, fell steadily until 1995 when there was an increase in numbers. It is too soon to tell whether the increase in the past two years signals a turning point, but it is possible that it may do so. Births outside marriage, which accounted for less than 2 per cent of total births in 1871, and less than 3 per cent of births in 1971, now account for one-quarter of all births, and one-third of all first births. Cohabitation is widespread. A new symbol of contemporary Ireland is the extent to which it is taken for granted that prominent people in public life may be accompanied by partners rather than spouses. Invitations are routinely addressed to 'Mr Murphy and guest', or sometimes to 'Ms Murphy and guest', rather than to 'Mr and Mrs Michael Murphy', as in yesteryear.

Experience of family life has differed hugely according to the level of family income and wealth. It was not the case in the last century that all families were impoverished peasant families, or later on, owner-occupiers of de Valera's idealised small family homesteads. In the post-famine years there were some well-to-do tenant farmers, like John O'Brien who rented two hundred acres in County Limerick and kept fifty dairy cows. His labourers 'were paid a shilling a day, which was threepence more than the wages usually given in the neighbourhood' (Carbery, 1937, p. 9). The subsistence tenant family of the 1850s with a brood of children, is a world apart from today's high-earning farm family, where one member of the couple may have off-farm employment, and the children third-level education. But today's high-earning farm family is also a world apart from the contemporary lone-parent family whose livelihood may depend on a social welfare payment and a rent allowance. The elements which most differentiated families 150 years ago, and indeed until the past twenty years when the distinction between marital and non-marital families has become important, were economic and class factors. The chasm between the family life of the Lord Lieutenant, or of any of the big landowners, and the wretched poverty of the west of Ireland peasant, was to all intents and purposes as great as that between the plantation owners of the southern states of the USA and their slaves.

For the ordinary people in the last century, and for a good part of this century, weddings together with wakes were not only the major, but almost the unique, social events of a lifetime. In his oral history of Dublin tenement life in the 1920s and 1930s, Kevin Kearns tells us:

> Wedding celebrations were held in the tenement room once beds had been removed to the hallway landing. Apart from a wedding cake there was usually a ham, corned beef and cabbage, potatoes and a big bowl of jelly for the wedding party. Sometimes just sandwiches had to suffice. But beer and whiskey were always brought over from the local pub. Music and dancing were part of the merriment as friends and neighbours drifted in and out of the scene. Usually the festivities spilled out into the street for all to enjoy. A lively wedding could last from a few days to a full week (Kearns, 1994, p. 47).

Moving up the social scale, weddings were much more grand affairs. A picture of a wedding cake, which incidentally symbolised much of contemporary values, appeared in *Model Housekeeping*, a popular women's magazine, in November 1934. It was the wedding cake of Mr Frank Aiken, Mr de Valera's right-hand man. The report that accompanied the picture was as follows:

> Mr Frank Aiken's Wedding Cake, made in Dundalk, his own constituency, weighed 110 lbs., stood 5 ft high and was artistically decorated with celtic interlacing in green and orange. Swords and crossguns, tiny green clad soldiers and musical instruments (in compliment to both bride and bridegroom) were some of the interesting features *(Model Housekeeping*, vol. VII, no. 1, November 1934).

Changes – data

A rich, and relatively untapped, source of information on family life, in all its diverse aspects, resides in autobiography and biography. From the point of view of understanding family change, works such as Mary Carbery's *The Farm by Lough Gur,* Tomas O'Criomhthain's *An t-Oileánach*, Peig Sayer's *Peig*, Mick McCarthy's *Early Days*, Elizabeth Fingall's *Seventy Years Young*, or in recent times, Gabriel Byrne's *Pictures in My Head*, Frank McCourt's *Angela's Ashes*, or Nuala O'Faolain's *'Are You Somebody?'*, yield a harvest of life and colour, tears and laughter, which statistics can never convey. The social contrasts remain extreme, almost as sharp as that between the innocent rural idyll of Alice Taylor in the 1940s and the fictional urban *The Family* of Roddy Doyle in the 1990s. In a different literary genre, probably no writer in Ireland this century has conveyed a starker picture of Irish family life than John McGahern, making an extraordinary contrast with the idealised life of the Irish tenant farmer and the farm worker in the nineteenth century – Mat the Thresher – in Kickham's *Knocknagow.*

The media also have much to tell us about change in family life. One example from television serves to illustrate. The first episode of *The Riordans* was screened on 4 January 1965 and the final episode on St Stephen's Day 1979. It continued for fifteen years and approximately five-hundred episodes. While the original intention was didactic – to encourage modernisation in farming – it led to a discussion on, and a questioning of, traditional values, especially those associated with rural family life. In the words of author Wesley Burrowes, the Riordan family comprised:

> Tom Riordan, a strong farmer; his wife Mary, absorbed in her family; one son Benjy just back from Agricultural College, waiting, not very patiently, for his chance to use his knowledge; the other son Michael at the University, studying to be an engineer. There is a daughter Angela, engaged to an Englishman of whom all the family are very wary. The younger sister Jude is a nurse in a Kilkenny hospital (Burrowes, 1977, p. 4).

The early programmes showed the interaction between characters, the strains between Benjy and his father, the peace-making role of Mary, and their relationships with neighbours. Gradually, as Luke Gibbons tells us, the serial brought to the surface 'with almost relentless zeal every possible transgression of the traditional Irish family enshrined in the 1937 Constitution' (Gibbons, 1984, p. 39). The list included illegitimacy; 'mixed marriage', that is marriage between those of different religions; adoption, 'mixed marriage' couples were prohibited from adopting children under the Adoption Act, 1952; marriage breakdown; divorce; cohabitation or 'living in sin'; and the idea of a 'kept woman'. Contraception also featured. Maggie, a barmaid, whose early life was spent in an orphanage, is married to Benjy Riordan. To quote Gibbons once more, when difficulties began to surface in Benjy's and Maggie's marriage:

> ... it became clear that the age of innocence had finally passed in representations of family and rural life in Ireland. The 1974 season revolved around the contentious issue of contraception, precipitated by Maggie's decision to go on the Pill, following the complications which attended the birth of her first child (Gibbons, 1984, p 41).

So what have been the biggest changes in family life in the past 150 years? Foremost has been the rise in the standard of living. Next has been the decline in mortality rates, in particular of mothers and infants. People in general are living much longer, with more elderly persons living alone or in homes separate from their families. In 1994 Ireland had the lowest maternal mortality in the world, with no deaths of women in childbirth in that year. At the foundation of the state there were close to 300 maternal deaths per year. This represented the death of a mother for approximately every 200 births.

For the years 1864 to 1870, when records were first kept, the average number of deaths of infants under one year exceeded 10,000, that is a rate of almost 10 per cent. The rate varied by area and by standard of housing. In 1926, for example, infant mortality was as high as 17 per cent in one area of Dublin. (Census 1926, *General Report*, p. 70). The infant mortality rate has fallen throughout the twentieth century to less than 1 per cent at present. Alongside the fall in infant mortality there has been a steady fall in the average number of children born per married woman, from approximately six to two. The number born to unmarried mothers has risen sharply.

Changes – roles

The decline in the number of marriages and births, the rapid growth in births outside marriage, the huge improvement in infant and maternal mortality rates, provide a broad framework of family change; the changes in the role of family members help to fill in the picture. The roles of men, women and children in family life have all changed significantly.

Studies of family change tend to focus a good deal on the changing role of women, but let's start with men. The term 'breadwinner' is important. It made its appearance in the Scottish census of 1871, which classified persons as earners and dependants, and the concept spread from there. With the growth of off-farm employment and the emergence of the 'working classes', the role of the man as breadwinner became central. The *Freeman's Journal* reported in 1907: 'The man who is worth his salt realises that his first duty is by the toil of his brains or his hands to make and keep a home for his wife and family. The woman can have no higher duty than to make that home happy' (quoted in Farmar, 1991).

Men who married were destined to become breadwinners for their wives and children. Character judgements were passed on men according to whether they were 'good providers', or not. For many years the tax and social welfare codes were based on the assumption that the family unit comprised a breadwinner father with dependent wife and children. In the modernisation phase, the 'breadwinner father' concept has been challenged on two fronts: the increasing economic independence of women, with more married women at work, and the growth in social welfare provision for lone parenthood, both of which have reduced the role of the breadwinner father. The scaling down of the breadwinner role has led to expressions of concern regarding the social consequences for men both in Ireland and elsewhere (Akerlof, 1998). At the same time there is a gathering movement among men to ensure that they play their full role, emotional and financial, in rearing their children. This trend is signalled, for example, in the work of social scientist, Kieran McKeown and journalist, John Waters.

Although on stage by the late nineteenth century, the role of 'housewife' is essentially a twentieth-century concept linked with industrial, rather than agrarian, society. Associated with the role of motherhood, the role of housewife is, nonetheless, distinct. 'Housewife' connotes a married woman whose life focuses almost exclusively on the home. She is responsible for the domestic realm. It is her job, although unpaid. She is the 'woman in the home' of the 1937 Constitution. By the end of the twentieth century, the housewife is moving off stage, with some feminist assistance. At present almost 40 per cent of married women are in the workforce and half of all families with children under 15 years are dual earner families (*Labour Force Survey*, 1997).

The housewife is distinct from the mother, and it is noteworthy that mothers are mentioned in the Constitution separately from the 'woman in the home'. Motherhood was highly valued by early feminists, including Eleanor Rathbone, author of *The Disinherited Family*, published in 1924. In order to ease the poverty of families, and desiring that mothering be judged worthy of financial reward, Rathbone urged a form of family benefit, to be paid to women. In Ireland, children's allowances were first introduced in 1944 for the third and each subsequent child and were gradually extended to all eligible children. In 1973, allowances were made payable to the mother, following a recommendation of the Commission on the Status of Women, chaired by Dr Thekla Beere.

The role and status of children has changed markedly. For much of the past 150 years it was considered both morally and financially wrong for children to be born outside marriage. The unmarried woman and her pregnancy were viewed as shameful. Many mothers and children suffered; sometimes the children were banished and lost all contact with their parents, and they were penalised under the law with regard to succession rights prior to the Status of Children Act, 1987.

The change in the economic position of children has been linked closely with two factors: the shift away from agriculture and the extension of compulsory education. From almost no official childhood in the last century, the years of dependency have been extended considerably in the late twentieth century. Until the late 1960s the majority of children left school after primary level. Well into the twentieth century, and especially in the small farm context, children were an important economic resource. Juveniles were employed in industry also. In the 1920s and 1930s women and girls predominated in the tobacco, sweet, chocolate and jam factories, as well as in tailoring, Jacob's biscuits and in several laundries.

The wider context

There is a tendency in Ireland to think that we are unique in family matters, and in a way we are. But every country has its own peculiarities. In mid-Victorian England almost one-third of the women aged between 20 and 44 years had to remain spinsters because the reservoir of men had been depleted by wars and migration to the colonies (Fox Harding, p. 48). In the late nineteenth century and for the first half of the twentieth century Irish patterns of marriage, births and labour force participation were out of line with the rest of Europe. On closer inspection what emerges is that the pace and timing of modernisation in Ireland differed considerably from the rest of Europe. For much of the twentieth century our demographic behaviour lagged behind; then in a short period from the late 1970s to the late 1980s Irish demographic behaviour was transformed.

In addition to differences in timing, what may be regarded as peculiarly Irish has been the tendency to deal with awkward problems, including divorce and abortion, by recourse to other countries. When capital punishment existed in Ireland, ordinary hangings, as distinct from military executions, were carried out by the English hangman, Pierpoint, who travelled to Ireland for the purpose. We did not have our own Irish hangman. It could, of course, be argued, that we did not have enough hangings to justify one, or we could call the tendency to export problems, the 'Pierpoint Syndrome'.

We live in a wider world and this was the case even in days when it was less obvious because international communications and travel were more limited. The idea that de Valera and the Catholic hierarchy – in particular the Catholic Archbishop of Dublin, Dr John Charles McQuaid – were, as a result of their study of Catholic teaching, largely responsible for the notion that a woman's place was exclusively in the home, and that they embedded this idea into the Irish Constitution of 1937, is not the whole truth. By the 1930s the industrialised world had reached the last stages of the demographic transition, which began around the 1870s, from high birth and death rates to a pattern of low birth and death rates. Throughout the 1930s, policies, forged by strong political ideologies, were put in place in a wide range of countries to encourage women to stay in the home and to rear children. In the 1970s, when the move to legalise contraceptives developed, and later in the 1990s, when separation and divorce laws were passed, Ireland was following the pattern of other European countries.

Throughout the countries of the EU, the increased number of elderly and the decline in births, and other family changes, have turned the attention of policy makers onto the family. Ireland is no exception. In October 1995, the government established a Commission of Inquiry on the Family under the chairmanship of Dr Michael Dunne. Its report will bring a new coherence into the amalgam of public policy areas that govern the state's interaction with families.

Looking back it would be as wrong to idealise the past as to condemn it. Family life has been experienced all along the income and wealth scale from poverty to affluence. Families at times have operated as secret societies in which individuals have been subjected to pain. It would also be mistaken to emphasise the changes to such a degree as to neglect strong underlying continuities. The family is a coat of many colours and changing styles.

REFERENCES

Akerlof, G.A. (1998), 'Men Without Children,' *The Economic Journal*, 108 (March), pp. 287–309

Burrowes, W. (1977), *The Riordans A Personal History*, Dublin: Gilbert Dalton

Carbery, M. (1937), *The Farm by Lough Gur*, London, New York, Toronto: Longmans, Green and Co.

Census of Population (1871), *General Report*

Census of Population (1926), *General Report*

Fanning, R. (1983), *Independent Ireland*, Dublin: Helicon

Farmar, T. (1991), *Ordinary Lives*, Dublin: A and A Farmar

Fox Harding, L. (1996), *Family, State and Social Policy*, Hampshire and London: Macmillan Press

Geary, R. C. (1935/36), 'The Future Population of Saorstát Éireann and Some Observations on Population Statistics', *Journal of the Statistical and Social Inquiry Society of Ireland*, vol. 15, session 89, 15–32

Gibbons, L. (1984), 'From Kitchen Sink to Soap: Drama and the Serial Form on Irish Television', in M. McLoone and J. MacMahon (eds.), *Television and Irish Society. 21 Years of Irish Television*, Dublin: RTE and Irish Film Institute

Kearns, K.C. (1994), *Dublin Tenement Life: An Oral History*, Dublin: Gill and Macmillan

Kennedy, F. and McCormack, K. (1997), 'Ireland – Marriage Loses Popularity', in F.X. Kaufman, A. Kuijsten, H.J. Schulze and P. Strohmeier (eds.), *Family Life and Family Policies in Europe*, vol. 1, Oxford: Clarendon Press

Labour Force Survey (1997)

Meenan, J. (1970), *The Irish Economy Since 1922*, Liverpool University Press

Model Housekeeping (1934), vol. VII, no. 1, November

Rathbone, E. (1924), *The Disinherited Family*, London: Edward Arnold

12

Constitutional and Legal Change

BLÁTHNA RUANE

The approach of the new millennium naturally prompts reflection on what progress has been made in the past along with some anticipation of the challenges awaiting us in the next millennium. I would like to give some personal reflections on the major changes that have occurred in the sphere of Irish constitutional law. I will attempt to sketch out the difference that having our own constitution has made to the operation of our legal system and how that difference has impacted on the lives of Irish people.

To consider these issues and set them in a wider perspective, it is useful to remind ourselves of where we started at the beginning of this century. At that stage Ireland was an integral part of the United Kingdom of Great Britain and Ireland and was ruled from Westminster. As part of the United Kingdom, Ireland did not have its own written constitution but functioned under the unwritten constitution of Great Britain. Under British constitutional theory parliament is supreme and the sovereignty of parliament effectively meant that parliament was able to change laws as and when it required to do so without constraint. Up until 1922 the absence of a clear written constitution protecting basic human rights had left Irish people particularly vulnerable to potentially serious incursions in the area of human rights by the Westminster parliament.

The 1922 Constitution

This changed with the signing of the Anglo-Irish Treaty in 1921. Its terms provided the basis for Irish independence. The

Treaty contained the most important provisions regulating the relationship between the new state and Great Britain. Ireland was to have dominion status with the King as head of state but did not have complete freedom.[1] The Treaty required members of the parliament of the Irish Free State to take an oath of allegiance to the King.[2] It also provided for an opt-out arrangement for Northern Ireland.[3] These arrangements within the Treaty itself were deeply offensive to many nationalists.

The Treaty also envisaged a formal act establishing a constitutional framework and this led to the enactment of a constitution. The Third Dáil, elected by the people in 1922, sat as a constituent assembly for the purpose of settlement of the Constitution of the Irish Free State. When the terms of the Constitution were finalised, it was introduced by means of the Irish Free State (Saorstát Éireann) Act of 1922. The 1922 Constitution, as it later came to be known, was subject to the terms of the Treaty which was made a schedule to it. Under Article 50 of the Constitution no amendment could be made to it which did not comply with the Treaty.

The Constitution established the essential tripartite division of powers between the legislature, executive and judiciary.[4] In addition, an important departure was its explicit protection of basic human rights, such as personal liberty,[5] freedom of religion[6] and trial by jury.[7] Another important innovation was the power given to the High Court to determine the validity of laws relative to the Constitution.[8] This meant that if the Oireachtas were to legislate in a manner inconsistent with the guaranteed rights, then that legislation could be invalidated by reference to the new Constitution.

The specific protection given to human rights in the 1922 Constitution did not live up to its potential. This was because of a provision within the Constitution itself [9] and some amendments made subsequently, which entitled the Oireachtas to amend the Constitution by means of legislation.[10] There was a challenge in the courts to this method of constitutional amendment but it failed.[11] The result was that the Oireachtas could legislate in ways which conflicted with the human rights guaranteed in the 1922 Constitution.

In retrospect one can see that the 1922 Constitution had a significant impact on several important aspects of Irish life. It provided a basic structure for the foundation of the new state. The establishment of the organs of government was the starting point for many changes within the legal system at that time and led to wide-ranging legislation establishing government departments, a new courts' system, the Garda Síochána and many other essential institutions for the newly emerging state. The structures adopted in the 1922 Constitution were largely successful and their form has been continued down to the present day albeit with some modifications. The 1922 Constitution had also recognised the principle that human rights should be explicitly protected in the Constitution and that courts should have the power to consider the validity of legislation by reference to those rights.

These were major achievements in a turbulent era when understandably the priority for the government, or executive council as it was then called, was the creation of a stable democracy. What is disappointing in retrospect is that subsequent changes to the Constitution had rendered its written protections for human rights ineffective. The experience of the 1922 Constitution showed that unless a constitution was relatively difficult to amend, its effectiveness as a guardian of individual rights could quickly be undermined.

The 1937 Constitution

De Valera came to power in 1932. He had long been unhappy with many aspects of the 1922 Constitution which epitomised the state's continuing lack of complete independence. He set about removing some sections of the 1922 Constitution by means of legislation[12] but ultimately he decided that an entirely new constitution should be introduced and he involved himself actively in its preparation.[13]

The result was the 1937 Constitution, *Bunreacht na hÉireann*, which was approved by the people. It bore many resemblances to its predecessor. The organs of government were largely the same,[14] with the addition of the office of president.[15] There was specific protection for human rights[16] and the courts continued to have a power to review legislation.[17] There were differences however. Gone were any references to the King and the Treaty. Indeed some elements of the new Constitution were at odds with the Treaty, particularly Articles 2 and 3 that defined the nature and extent of the state in a way which included Northern Ireland.

The role of the courts in determining the constitutional validity of legislation was strengthened by allowing the President to refer bills to the Supreme Court.[18] The protection afforded to fundamental rights was considerably expanded. The tone of the Constitution was also significantly different in that it was far less secular than the 1922 Constitution had been. A strong theistic, nationalistic element ran through it, particularly clear in the content of the Preamble. Some of the rights were expressed in terms indicating that they derived from natural law.[19] The influence of the Roman Catholic Church was evident in that the special position of that church was acknowledged.[20] For the first time there was a specific prohibition on divorce.[21] Another important difference was that this time the Constitution could only be amended by ordinary legislation for a period of three years and the three-year period could not be extended.[22] Thereafter a referendum would be required for any change.[23] This was a clear break with the 1922 Constitution and was of critical importance in establishing the role of the Constitution as a more permanent fixture, which could only be changed by the people.

It was not really envisaged at the time of its introduction that *Bunreacht na hÉireann* was going to impinge on the daily life of the nation in the way that was to occur later. Parts of the Constitution were probably perceived as being almost aspirational in nature, rather than being the source of concrete rights that could be enforced in courts of law. Initially it appeared that the 1937 Constitution would prove ineffective in protecting human rights. This was because of an important decision given in early 1940 in which the Supreme Court upheld the Offences Against the State (Amendment) Bill of 1940.[24] In the process it gave a very restrictive interpretation of some of the fundamental rights provisions of the new Constitution. That decision severely dampened, for many years, any hope that the new Constitution would be an important source of human rights protection and thereafter there were few constitutional cases brought until the 1960s when that restrictive outlook began to change.

Judicial development

Probably many factors combined to produce what in retrospect was a dramatic change in attitude towards the Constitution. There were broad social changes as Ireland became less insular and there was a heightened international awareness of the importance of human rights. These wide influences helped to create greater expectations of what the Constitution could achieve for Irish society. However, a receptive judiciary was critical to concrete realisation of those changing constitutional values.

It was fortunate that just when these general changes were taking place, there were people at the top of the Irish legal system who were outward looking and imaginative enough to respond to these changes. Cearbhaill Ó Dalaigh became Chief Justice in 1963 and he oversaw a major change in attitude to the Constitution. He was invaluably assisted in creating these changes by Mr Justice Brian Walsh, Mr Justice Gardner Budd, Mr Justice Seamus Henchy and Mr Justice John Kenny. The new approach was that the Constitution was there to be enforced and the courts' powers were as ample as the defence of the Constitution required.

In 1964 the Supreme Court decided that it would not be rigidly bound by previous decisions but could depart from them for compelling reasons.[25] This signalled a new openness in attitude. Shortly afterwards another important development was the recognition for the first time of unspecified rights under Article 40.3 of the Constitution.[26] The court held that the rights listed in Article 40.3 were not exhaustive and that there was a category of latent, unspecified personal rights, which were also protected by the Constitution. This undid the stultifying interpretation of the same Article given by the Supreme Court in 1940. Article 40.3 has since become a major repository for the identification of unrecognised personal rights. Many of these rights have been associated with important social issues, such as the right to bodily integrity,[27] marital privacy,[28] individual privacy,[29] the rights of the child,[30] the right to legal representation on criminal charges[31] and the right to fair procedures.[32]

Family law and the right to life

Changes occurred in all areas of constitutional law. A few examples will illustrate the impact. The sphere of what might loosely be called family law, for example, has seen huge change. In 1973 the Supreme Court in *McGee v Attorney General*[33] held that the banning of the sale and importation of contraceptives infringed the right to marital privacy. This was a dramatic change since earlier attempts to introduce legislation to liberalise the law on contraception had failed. The 1968 papal encyclical *Humane Vitae* had prohibited the use of artificial contraceptives even by married couples. It was an issue that undoubtedly was difficult for the legislators to confront. The outcome of the decision demonstrated the broadening relevance of the Constitution and its role in effecting change.

In 1978 in *G. v An Bord Uchtála*[34] the right of a natural mother of a non-marital child to the custody of her child was identified as another unenumerated right, and the rights of children to proper protection and education were also recognised. The right of a married couple to procreate was recognised in 1985.[35] A decision given in 1989 upheld the constitutionality of legislation providing for the adoption of a child of a marital family who had been abandoned by both parents.[36]

Probably the most far reaching constitutional change affecting the family took place not as a result of constitutional adjudication by the courts but by referendum, namely the removal of the absolute ban on divorce, which occurred in 1995. Divorce is now possible but only in limited circumstances and where a marriage has been irretrievably broken down for a specified period.

One area of change that has proved particularly traumatic is that relating to the right to life and in particular the right to life of the unborn. The trauma produced by the abortion issue demonstrates that amendment and interpretation of the Constitution can be an extremely difficult process, and the results unpredictable. It will be recalled that in 1983 the Constitution was amended to insert a provision, Article 40.3.3, whereby the state acknowledged the right to life of the unborn and, with due regard to the equal right to life of the mother, guaranteed in its laws to respect and, as far as practicable by its laws, to defend and vindicate that right. In 1992 in the *X case* the Supreme Court was first called upon to interpret Article 40.3.3 in circumstances involving a fourteen-year-old school girl, who was pregnant as a result of an alleged rape and who had threatened suicide.[37] The girl wished to travel to England to have an abortion. The court held that the right to life of the unborn had to be balanced against the mother's right to life. It held that the Article permitted termination of a pregnancy in the state when there was a real and substantial threat to the mother's life as distinct from her health. It also concluded that the threat of suicide constituted a threat to the mother's life for that purpose. While the decision allowed the girl to travel, some statements of the majority of the court indicated that the constitutional right to travel under domestic law could be restrained so as to prevent an abortion taking place abroad when there was no threat to the mother's life.

The decision gave rise to intense debate culminating in a further amendment to the Constitution in 1993 confirming freedom to travel to use an abortion service lawfully operating elsewhere and freedom to obtain or make available information relating to such services subject to conditions provided by law. There was also an attempt to amend the original wording inserted in 1983 dealing with the substantive issue in terms which would have rendered abortion more difficult to procure in the state and would have specifically precluded suicide as a ground for obtaining an abortion. That amendment was defeated and so the availability of abortion is governed by the wording of the 1983 amendment as interpreted by the Supreme

Court in the *X case* and which was followed more recently in the *C case*.[38]

Considerable controversy remains over the substantive issue and may lead to a further referendum at some stage. In the meantime no legislation has yet been introduced to regulate the availability of abortion within the state. In the absence of such legislation, there remains considerable uncertainty about the meaning of Article 40.3.3, such as what is the time limit for a lawful termination of a pregnancy, how to determine whether there is a real and substantial risk to the life of the mother and who should make that decision. There is still no clear procedure that will protect medical staff who may be called upon in very difficult circumstances to provide medical treatment.

Other developments

Apart from family issues, there have been many other well-publicised constitutional developments, such as those relating to property rights, freedom of religion, the rights of an accused and of prisoners, freedom of association and rights to education. However, there have also been other less well-publicised developments since the 1960s, which have actually had considerable impact on the ordinary life of the citizen. These have included the recognition of the principle of constitutional justice, which requires that proper procedures be observed in the making of decisions or taking of actions affecting an individual's constitutional rights.[39]

Another subtle development, which has received little public attention, was the determination that legislation has to be implemented in a way which respects the Constitution.[40] So, for example, even where the Oireachtas in enacting legislation which affects constitutional rights, did not provide specific protection for those rights, the legislation nonetheless has to be interpreted and implemented, so far as possible, in a way which respects those rights. Otherwise it would be regarded as being unconstitutional. Constitutional protections are, as it were, read into the legislation automatically. This has meant that on a day-to-day basis government departments and other statutory bodies have had to change how they operate and ensure that the way they exercise powers respects the citizen's constitutional rights. These are changes that are not confined to any one aspect of life but impact right across the board.

Another profound change that has occurred is the extent to which the individual is able to exert a tangible measure of control over actions of the government even in areas of high public interest. This was shown vividly in 1987, in *Crotty v An Taoiseach*, when the Supreme Court decided that even where the Constitution gave the government exclusive power in the conduct of external relations, the courts could restrain the government from acting inconsistently with the Constitution.[41] The Supreme Court concluded that Title 3 of the Single European Act was unconstitutional, which meant that the government could not deposit the instruments of ratification of the Single European Act. A referendum was needed to amend the Constitution to allow the state to ratify it.

A more recent example of an individual's usage of the Constitution to control governmental action was the McKenna decision in 1995.[42] There the Supreme Court concluded that the government had acted in breach of the Constitution in expending public monies in exclusively promoting a yes vote in the referendum on the removal of the constitutional prohibition on divorce. These examples show that a member of the public can exert a measure of restraining control over governmental action even in spheres of high public interest. Years ago the idea of individuals being able to keep a government in check in such instances would have been unthinkable.

The continuing work of the courts in considering the constitutionality of legislation in areas of social importance has itself become a vehicle of social change. Bringing constitutional cases, whether successful or not, can be used by individuals and lobby groups to publicise an issue and pressurise politicians to make changes. Even a crude statistical exercise provides an indication of the extent to which the Constitution is increasingly invoked. In the 1926 volume of the *Irish Reports*, covering the more important Irish legal cases, there were five constitutional cases. By 1996 the figure had risen to fourteen. The practical impact of this focus on the Constitution has been to make the task of legislating far more onerous. In producing draft bills, governments must now consider a wide variety of issues that may affect their constitutionality.

Constitutional amendment

Of course, apart from judicial development, the Constitution has also been developed by amendment through referendum on many occasions. The more important amendments concerned Ireland's membership of the EEC and the various developments that ensued with the Single European Act and the Maastricht Treaty; the amendments dealing with the removal of the special position of the Catholic Church; the right to life; the right to travel and information; the removal of the absolute ban on divorce; and more recently, the right to bail; and cabinet confidentiality. It is clear that the Irish public has become increasingly aware of the relevance and importance of its Constitution and expects a high level of debate and availability of information about the issues involved prior to a referendum vote.

The Constitution is not the only yardstick against which national legislation is now measured. Ireland's membership of the European Union means that, in the relevant areas, its national legislation must not offend European law and this has resulted in an additional layer of scrutiny of legislation. Constitutional jurisprudence has in the process become influenced by the jurisprudence of the European Court of Justice. In addition, the jurisprudence of the European Court of Human Rights in Strasbourg now carries considerable influence in Irish courts despite the fact that the European Convention on Human Rights is still not enforceable in national law. At the same time English common law and American constitutional decisions remain very influential. These external legal influences operate as a modernising force on the development of Irish constitutional law.

Conclusion

The rapid developments of the last thirty-five years have shown that the Constitution has largely operated successfully. Overall the 1937 Constitution has stood the test of time remarkably well and the fact that the Constitution is capable of amendment by the people has been an important element in ensuring its continuing relevance and ability to reflect the changing values in Irish society. The fact that it can only be amended by the people has also meant that it cannot be changed too readily and only after public debate. It has also had the healthy effect of re-enforcing in everyone's minds that it is the people who determine its contents. It emphasises the democratic nature of the state and the fact that it is not the state which controls the people but rather the people who control the state.

As greater social diversity develops, so there will be more pressure upon the Constitution to provide adequate protections for all of the differing and competing values that will emerge. There are areas of the Constitution where amendment would be worthwhile. To date the changes have been piecemeal but there have been suggestions for more wide-scale changes. The Constitution Review Group, under the chairmanship of Dr T.K. Whitaker, gave a comprehensive report in May 1996 suggesting a wide variety of amendments and the All-Party Oireachtas Committee continues the review process. What amendments may result from this consideration remain to be seen.

What is clear, however, is that a well-educated Irish electorate has an increasingly sophisticated understanding of constitutional issues and expects careful and informed debate about any proposed changes. Some proposals for change may raise very difficult issues. In facing the challenges that such debates will bring, we should remember that we have already achieved a great deal in a very short period. That success should be a source of confidence to us in facing the constitutional challenges that lie ahead in the next millennium.

NOTES

1 Articles 1–3

2 Article 4

3 Articles 11–15

4 Articles 2, 12–48, 51–59, 64–69

5 Article 6

6 Article 8

7 Article 72

8 Article 65

9 Article 50

10 These are described and discussed in *The State (Ryan) v Lennon* [1935] I.R. 170

11 *The State (Ryan) v Lennon* [1935] I.R. 170

12 For example, The Constitution (Removal of Oath) Act 1933, The Constitution (Amendment No. 20) Act 1933 and The Constitution (Amendment No. 21) Act 1933

13 The background is described in D. Keogh 'The Irish Constitutional Revolution: An Analysis of the Making of the Constitution', in F. Litton (ed.) 'The Constitution of Ireland', *Administration*, vol. 35, 1988, Dublin: IPA, p. 4; and G. Hogan 'The Constitution Review Committee of 1934' in F. Ó Muircheartaigh (ed.) *Ireland in the Coming Times: Essays to Celebrate T.K. Whitaker's 80 Years*, Dublin: IPA (1997), p. 342

14 Articles 6, 15–27, 28, 34–38

15 Articles 12–14

16 Articles 40–44

17 Articles 15.4 and 34.3.2

18 Article 26

19 For example, Article 41.1

20 Article 44.1.2,3

21 Article 41.3.2

22 Article 51.1 (Transitory Provision)

23 Article 46

24 [1940] I.R. 470

25 *Attorney General v Ryan's Car Hire Limited* [1965] I.R. 642

26 *Ryan v Attorney General* [1965] I.R. 294

27 *Ryan v Attorney General* [1965] I.R. 294

28 *McGee v Attorney General* [1974] I.R. 284

29 *Kennedy v Ireland* [1987] I.R. 587

30 In re *Article 26 and the Adoption (No. 2) Bill 1987*, [1989] I.R. 656; *G. v An Bord Uchtála* [1980] I.R. 32

31 *The State (Healy) v Donoghue* [1971] I.R. 217

32 In re *Haughey* [1971] I.R. 217

33 [1974] I.R. 284

34 [1980] I.R. 32

35 *Murray v Ireland* [1985] I.R. 532

36 In re *Article 26 and the Adoption (No. 2) Bill 1987*, [1989] I.R. 656

37 *Attorney General v X & Ors.* [1992] 1 I.R. 1

38 *A. and B. v Eastern Health Board, Judge Mary Fahy and C.* [unreported, High Court, Geoghegan J., 28 November 1997]

39 *Glover v BLN* [1973] I.R. 388; *The State (Gleeson) v Minister for Defence* [1976] I.R. 280

40 *East Donegal Co-Operative v Attorney General* [1970] I.R. 317

41 *Crotty v An Taoiseach* [1987] I.R. 713

42 *McKenna v An Taoiseach* (No. 2) [1995] 2 I.R. 10

FURTHER READING

There are excellent general texts on Irish constitutional law such as G. Hogan and G. Whyte (eds.), *J.M. Kelly – The Irish Constitution*, Dublin and London: Butterworths, 3rd edition, 1994; and J. Casey, *Constitutional Law in Ireland*, London: Sweet and Maxwell, 2nd edition, 1992. The *Report of the Constitution Review Group* (Dublin: Stationery Office, May 1996), considered possible amendments of the Constitution in the light of developments in Ireland generally. Other works of interest include *De Valera's Constitution and Ours*, B. Farrell (ed.), Dublin: Gill and Macmillan 1988 (the *Thomas Davis Lecture Series* given to mark the fiftieth anniversary of the introduction of *Bunreacht na hÉireann*) and 'The Constitution of Ireland 1937–1987', F. Litton (ed.), *Administration*, vol. 35, Dublin: IPA, 1988.

13

Crime and Punishment

CHARLES LYSAGHT

One side effect of the Great Famine of the 1840s was an escalation in the rate of crime. There were 300 homicides per year between 1845 and 1850, a figure, relative to population, never subsequently approached let alone equalled. A record number of between 2,000 and 3,000 were transported annually in these years to penal colonies in the Australias. In 1850, 10,000 prisoners languished in Irish gaols. But, after the boil of overpopulation had been lanced so brutally by starvation, cholera, and the departure of a million starving people to other lands, Irish society settled down to a period of relative tranquillity that some were to look back upon as a golden age. Although the magazine *Punch* and other English commentators saw Ireland as a lawless land, there was, in fact, considerably less crime per head of population in Ireland than in England in the years between the Famine and the First World War. There was, it must be said, more agrarian crime, especially during the Land War of the 1880s. One effect of political unrest, of which this agrarian crime was a manifestation, was that Ireland, especially rural Ireland, was more heavily policed than other parts of the United Kingdom. This probably acted as a brake on criminal activities as did a better organised clergy, who had established themselves firmly as community leaders controlling the lives of the people from whom they sprang.

While, in the words of one contemporary observer of post-famine Ireland, there was less theft and crime indicating a low moral tone than elsewhere in the United Kingdom, assaults were more prevalent. Convictions for drunkenness rose steadily. They reached an annual figure of 100,000 around the turn of the century. Until 1914 the rate of homicide remained at a level that was not to be reached again until the closing decades of this century. But a significant number of the victims were babies, killed by their unfortunate mothers shortly after birth.

Crime in the new Irish state

After the intermittent lawlessness of the period between the Easter Rebellion of 1916 and the end of the Civil War in 1923, there was some apprehension that the new Irish Free State would not turn out to be a very law-abiding place. Official reports voiced fears about half-educated youths who had escaped early from parental control and grown up in lawless habits, with the streets and the cinemas as the main sources of their moral education. In fact, crime settled at a level that was in some significant respects much lower than it had been before the First World War. The number of assaults moved steadily downwards. So did homicides. They fell from eighteen per million in 1905 to ten per million in 1939 and four per million between 1949 and 1969. Convictions for drunkenness diminished dramatically. There was, on the other hand, more larceny and burglary. But the increase was of modest proportions and almost entirely concentrated in Dublin and a few other major urban centres. (This pattern was sustained into the years after the Second World War.) It was, it must be remembered, a society where the restless young, the segment of the population from whom criminals were most likely to be recruited, emigrated in their tens of thousands every year. Those who showed criminal propensities were sometimes granted leniency if they did just this.

The low level of crime was the good side of the coin, the other side of which was stagnation and hypocrisy. Throughout most of the country the Garda Síochána were left to concern themselves largely with drinking after hours, unlit bicycles, motoring offences, and the odd cases of poaching and poteen making, all crimes that involved little moral opprobrium. The staple diet of the Circuit Court, which tried most serious crimes other than murder, was charges of unlawful carnal knowledge of young females, especially after the age of consent was raised from sixteen to seventeen in 1935, largely as a gesture to the political correctness of that period.

The rise in crime since the 1960s

Whatever its causes, this policeman's paradise came to an end in the mid-1960s when Ireland lost its uniqueness and, in this as in other ways, it stepped forward two generations in one and moved closer to the model of other developed countries. There has been a large increase in all forms of serious crime. The largest increase has been in burglaries, robberies and drug offences. Reported burglaries, which had numbered less than 3,000 in 1960, rose to 36,000 in 1984; the number of robberies rose from 40 to 2,100 over the same period. Other forms of theft increased fivefold. After 1984, crimes against property generally levelled out but robberies, mainly muggings, continued to rise. Reported sexual assaults have more than trebled since 1990 reflecting, at least in part, a greater willingness of victims to complain to the police. A significant increase in murders, to over 40 per year, was recorded in 1995 and 1996. But this, it should be noted, did no more than bring the per capita rate of murder into line with that in Great Britain. The general level of crime remains significantly below that in Great Britain and other West European countries and is minuscule compared with that in the United States of America.

The causes of this epidemic of crime have been variously identified as deprivation, unemployment, social change, urbanisation, the decline in religious belief and moral standards, broken families, drugs, improved communications, television, the stimulations of advertising, and the conflict in Northern Ireland. While most detected crime has been committed by those who could be termed socially disadvantaged, there is reason to believe that there have been increased levels of white-collar crime, which is still little prosecuted. A feature of crime in recent decades is that about half of those convicted of the more serious categories of offences, known as indictable offences, are under 21 years of age. This age group accounted for only one-third of such offences in the middle years of the century and an even lower proportion before the First World War. On the other hand female offenders who accounted for one-third of such offences in those days now account for less than 15 per cent of them.

Changing approaches to punishment

Until the early nineteenth century those convicted of most felonies were liable to be executed. Felonies so punishable included larceny of anything over one shilling in value, as well as more serious crimes, such as arson, robbery, rape and murder, therefore death sentences were commonplace. In practice, they were often commuted and such reprieved convicts were transported to penal settlements, first in the Americas and then in Australia. Minor offenders, who were not whipped or fined, received short prison sentences. They were congregated into gaols for which local justices were responsible but which were often farmed out to be run by private individuals. While well-off prisoners might live in the lap of luxury in such establishments, the generality of inmates huddled together in squalor and hunger. Little was done to segregate child offenders from others. All manner of corruption was rife.

By the middle of the nineteenth century the death penalty had, effectively, been confined to those convicted of murder. Transportation was abandoned shortly after 1850 as it was no longer acceptable to the Australians. A sentence called penal servitude was substituted for it. It consisted of imprisonment for three years or more served in special convict prisons established at Mountjoy in Dublin, Maryborough in the Queen's County, Spike Island and Lusk. Each convict had a separate cell and was not allowed to associate with other inmates. Rations were sparse and there was a grinding regime of compulsory unproductive labour. In Ireland as in other parts of the United Kingdom prisons were now better regulated; in 1878 all Irish prisons were brought under the control of the General Prisons Board for Ireland and a uniform regime established. Conditions in them reflected a determination that inmates should not enjoy a more comfortable way of life than those living in poverty outside. The result was harsh. As Oscar Wilde wrote in the *Ballad of Reading Gaol*:

> Each narrow cell in which we dwell
> Is a foul and dark latrine

If imprisonment in the Victorian age was designed to punish and deter, it also contained within it elements of rehabilitation. Chaplains were employed to urge prisoners to seek God's forgiveness for their misdeeds and to turn from their sinful ways. Sir Walter Crofton, the first chairman of the Irish Convict Prisons Board in the 1850s, instituted the famous Intermediate System. Under this convicts were gradually reintegrated into the community towards the end of their sentences before obtaining total release on a 'ticket-of-leave' conditional upon good behaviour. Crofton's experiment was much admired and was copied in other countries. Rehabilitation was also assisted by prison-visiting and care of prisoners after release, both of which became recognised forms of charitable work.

Concern for children caught up in crime led to the creation of reformatories for child offenders; the first Irish reformatory was opened at Glencree in 1858 on a site donated by Lord Powerscourt. A later development for slightly older offenders was borstal, so-called because it was pioneered in a village of that name in Kent. Its stated object was to inculcate in the inmates a spirit of manliness and self-reliance approximating to that which obtained in the English public schools. The system was to be immortalised in the title of Brendan Behan's book *The Borstal Boy*. In this the writer records several relatively happy years spent in borstal in England after he had been apprehended as a 16 year-old on his way to plant bombs on the eve of the Second World War. An Irish borstal was established in Clonmel under the management of the Rosminian Fathers in 1908.

When imprisonment was substituted for death as the penalty for serious crimes, sentencing became more a matter of judicial discretion. While maximum penalties fixed by parliament gave guidance, the variety of conduct encompassed by particular crimes was such that it was seldom feasible to have a fixed or a minimum penalty. The practice was established that the prosecutor did not suggest a sentence. Nor did juries although they might occasionally add a rider to a verdict of 'guilty' in which they recommended leniency, especially in cases where the death penalty might be imposed. The individual judges who imposed sentences were not required to give reasons for their decisions. There was no appeal. All this made it difficult to achieve consistency in sentencing. Despite the introduction of an appeals system, this remains a besetting problem of the criminal justice system to this day.

In Ireland before independence very short prison sentences were common. As late as 1910, 30 per cent of those committed to prison had been sentenced to less than a week's imprisonment. In their report for that year the General Prisons Board remarked that over 9,000 persons had been committed for drunkenness and protested that they had frequently called attention to the uselessness of sending habitual drunkards to prison. The heavy use of imprisonment by courts reflected the lack of alternative punishments available to them. Corporal punishment remained on the statute book for certain offences, such as robbery with violence and for young offenders, but it was used very sparingly; the Judicial Statistics for 1869 reveal only four cases of whipping that year. Fines were not of much use because many offenders lacked the means to pay them and ended up in prison.

Attitudes to the treatment of offenders

The treatment of offenders was a constant preoccupation of the Statistical and Social Inquiry Society of Ireland from the time of its foundation in 1847. In 1911 Lord Justice Cherry read a paper to it on juvenile crime and its prevention. He recalled a case tried a hundred years previously where a young girl had been executed for stealing a piece of ribbon to adorn her hair. "One can scarcely now realise", he remarked, "the cruelty and heartlessness with which young criminals were treated until the middle of the last century. I have every hope", he concluded, with the faith in human progress so typical of those days, "that by careful reformatory treatment of every case of juvenile crime, combined with proper means being adopted to secure honest employment for those who have gone through it, we can entirely get rid of the criminal class in our big cities". In 1920 Thomas Molony, a north-side Dubliner educated by the Christian Brothers at North Richmond Street, who was the last Lord Chief Justice of Ireland under the Union, addressed the Society on the prevention and punishment of crime. "In order to impose the proper sentence", he said, "a judge should make himself acquainted with the principles of prison administration, and should himself visit prisons and other penal institutions from time to time." He himself was a regular prison visitor and was an active member of the Discharged Prisoners' Aid Society. It was an impressive legacy of involvement for the judges of the independent Irish state that came into existence two years later.

All the existing forms of criminal punishment were inherited by that state. There were twenty-seven executions of persons convicted of murder by the civil courts between 1924 and 1953. An English hangman had to be imported to perform the task. According to one of the characters in Brendan Behan's play *The Quare Fellow* there was no Irish hangman because it was stated in the advertisement for the post that he must be a fluent Irish speaker and no suitable applications were received. Behan's play, first performed in 1956, was based on an execution that took place while he was a prisoner in Mountjoy during the Second World War. It is a powerful indictment of the death penalty and depicts its harrowing effects on all those involved. It was also a disadvantage of capital punishment that it made juries reluctant to convict an accused, even if there was compelling evidence of guilt. In 1964 the death penalty was abolished for all except very restricted categories of murder, such as that of a policeman or a diplomat. Although several members of the Garda Síochána were murdered in the succeeding years none of those convicted was executed. The death penalty was abolished totally in 1990. Corporal punishment also fell into complete disuse long before its final removal from the statute book in 1996.

Imprisonment and the prisons

Conditions of imprisonment were improved in the decades after independence in line with what was happening in England. The solitary confinement, unproductive work and absence of mattresses that had been part of the regime for those sentenced to penal servitude or imprisonment with hard labour disappeared. This signified an acceptance of the principle that criminals were sent to prison as a punishment, not for punishment. It was consistent with this new emphasis that from the 1940s onwards prisoners were allowed magazines and radio, recreation in association with one another, smoking and the right to wear their own clothes. In the 1960s technical instruction and courses of education were introduced.

Committals to prison, which had been moving gradually downwards between 1880 and 1914, fell dramatically in the years after independence. In 1928 there were less than 4,000 committals to prison in the Free State compared with 29,000 in 1910 and over 40,000 in 1878 for the whole island. Even when allowance is made for the presence of one-third of the population of the island in Northern Ireland, where the crime rate was higher, this represented a substantial reduction in the number of prison sentences. In their last report before their abolition in 1928, the General Prisons Board commented:

> Among the most important factors which contributed to the considerable decrease in the prison population during the last half century must be reckoned the Probation of First Offenders Act, 1887, the Fines or Imprisonment Act, 1899 (which provided for reduction of sentences on part payment of fines), the Prisons Act, 1907 (which authorised partial remission of sentences for good conduct and industry) and the provisions of the Criminal Justice Administration Act, 1914 allowing time for payment of fines.

More and more it became the practice not to send first offenders to prison except for very serious offences. In deciding on sentence, especially in the case of a young person, judges were willing to look beyond retribution and to take account of what would be conducive to the rehabilitation of the offender.

This greater leniency may be viewed as a reaction to a reduction in the number of offences against the person . It could also be attributed to having judges who were less English in culture and so disposed to be less severe on crimes of dishonesty and those where intoxication was involved. By the 1950s the number of committals annually had fallen further to 1,500, while the average prison population had reached an all-time low of less than 500.

The huge rise in crime that began in the mid-1960s was reflected in the numbers sent to prison. In 1995 almost 6,000 persons were committed to prison compared with less than 3,000 in 1970 and 1,900 in 1960. But dramatic though these increases were, they fell far short of matching the increase in crime. There were several reasons for this. An expanded probation service and the juvenile liaison scheme operated by the Garda Síochána gave courts the option of placing offenders under supervision in the community rather than sending them to prison. After 1984, offenders who would otherwise have merited imprisonment could be ordered to do up to 240 hours work under supervision on socially useful projects. More problematically, space was created for incoming prisoners by releasing other prisoners long before they had served their full sentence. The revolving door syndrome so created was a sloppy expedient of the kind often dubbed 'an Irish solution to an Irish problem'. It represented an arbitrary interference with judicial decisions, which was all the more objectionable because no public notice was given of such releases.

The prison system has been consistently under-resourced. Conditions in Irish prisons have been condemned as primitive by a succession of inquiries, both domestic and international. Overcrowding has led to doubling up in cells, so reversing one of the major reforms of the nineteenth century. Drugs and suicides have become regular features of prison life. Rehabilitative schemes involving productive work, technical instruction and education have been largely undermined. One would probably have to go back to the early nineteenth century to find a time when prisons were as corrupting for those incarcerated in them. Recidivism, or repeat offending, by those who have served prison sentences has remained a major problem. The situation has been exacerbated because former prisoners have found it difficult to find employment and therefore have tended to drift back to crime. Instead of recognising that a prisoner who has served a sentence has paid his debt to society and actively assisting their rehabilitation, the state has treated them as ineligible for employment by it. A noteworthy feature of the prison population in recent decades is that only about 2 per cent are female, despite the fact that almost 15 per cent of those convicted have been women. This reflects a growing disinclination to impose prison sentences for prostitution, drunkenness and shoplifting, the crimes most often committed by women.

The major alternative form of punishment: the fine, has been plagued by executive interference as insidious as the early release of prisoners. From the middle of this century a practice grew up by which ministers for justice remitted fines wholesale, often as a political favour and always without any public notification. It was not until 1995 that this practice was curbed and then only as a result of a public-spirited action brought by Patrick Brennan, a retired judge of the District Court in Mayo, who was understandably indignant at this arbitrary interference with his considered decisions. A large percentage of fines have not been collected. At the same time a sizeable number of fine defaulters have ended up in prison, no action having been taken on recommendations that confiscation rather than imprisonment is the appropriate remedy when fines are not paid. Motoring offences, which are the majority of all offences, have almost invariably been punished by fines, supplemented by disqualification in some cases. But the fine has been rendered largely ineffective as a sanction for these and other offences, even where the offender has the means to pay, because maximum fines have been fixed at too low a level or have not been adjusted upwards in line with inflation. That those responsible for the criminal justice system have been so indifferent to a means by which this system could make a meaningful contribution to its own funding is symptomatic of the myopia that has affected it.

A Committee of Inquiry into the Penal System under the chairmanship of Dr T.K. Whitaker, which reported in 1985, argued that imprisonment should be used less, especially for offences against property not involving violence. They have been supported by eminent criminologists. However, a political consensus has emerged favouring greater severity. This has been fuelled by vocal lobbies representing victims. Public opinion surveys have revealed substantial support for longer sentences and even for the reintroduction of corporal punishment. Although judges may have become more reluctant to impose prison sentences, they have tended to impose longer sentences on those they send to prison; there were 550 sentences of imprisonment in excess of two years in 1995 compared with 30 in 1970. This may reflect what the Director of Public Prosecutions has described as 'the appalling increase in the nastiness of crimes of violence'. But it also betokens an increased severity of sentencing, which has been most noticeable in the case of sexual offences. Maximum sentences have been increased for a number of offences. A mandatory minimum prison sentence, unknown in modern times except for murder and treason, has been proposed by the government for those convicted of supplying forbidden drugs. Despite the prohibitive cost, in the region of £50,000 per prisoner per year, prison places are being expanded above 2,500, which was the average prison population before the First World War.

Rehabilitation

It is also possible to detect a definite shift in the prevailing philosophy of punishment. While there are programmes in prison to aid rehabilitation, especially for drug offenders and sex offenders, less has been heard in recent years of the likelihood of rehabilitation as a reason for imposing more lenient sentences, even on the young. In 1996 the Law Reform Commission rejected rehabilitation as a proper consideration for a judge to take into account when deciding on severity of sentence, It recommended that offenders should always receive their 'just desserts', measured by reference to their moral culpability and to the harm that they have done. While the sense of right and wrong that underlay the Victorian doctrine of retribution may have receded, the need for self-protection has injected a new harshness into attitudes towards criminal punishment that may not yet have run its full course.

This harshness may be understandable as a reaction when, after over a century of social and penal reform, society finds itself faced with a relentless wave of crime. But raw repression, we should remember, has been tried before as a method of eliminating crime and has not succeeded. It may be that more severity is called for in certain spheres, such as white-collar crime. But on both moral and practical grounds, it would be regrettable if severity were accepted as an alternative to a renewed emphasis on the goals of rehabilitating offenders and getting to grips with the root causes of delinquency in our society. These goals, based on the conviction that we must not reject the sinner even if we reject the sin, have been the inspiration of much laudable social and penal reform over the last 150 years.

FURTHER READING

Brewer, J. et al. (1997), Crime in Ireland, 1945–95, Oxford: Clarendon Press

Cherry, R.R. (1910–11), 'Juvenile Crime and its Prevention', *Journal of the Statistical and Social Inquiry Society of Ireland*, vol. 12, 435–50

Dooley, E. (1995), *Homicide in Ireland 1972–1991*, Dublin: Department of Justice

Henry, B. (1994), *Dublin Hanged: Crime, Law Enforcement and Punishment in Eighteenth Century Dublin*, Dublin: The Round Hall Press

Hinde, R.S.E. (1977), 'Sir Walter Crofton and the Reform of the Irish Convict System', *Irish Jurist*, vol. XII (New Series), 115–47, 295–337

McCullagh, C. (1996), *Crime in Ireland: A Sociological Introduction*, Cork: Cork University Press

McDowell, R.B. (1964), *The Irish Administration 1801–1914*, London: Routledge and Kegan Paul

McGowan, J. (1978) 'Nineteenth-Century Developments in Irish Prison Administration', *Administration,* vol. 26, 496–508, Dublin: IPA

Molony, T. (1920–1921), 'The Prevention and Punishment of Crime', *Journal of the Statistical and Social Inquiry Society of Ireland*, vol. 14, 117–32

O'Mahony, P. (1993), *Crime and Punishment in Ireland*, Dublin: The Round Hall Press

O'Mahony, P. (1996), *Criminal Chaos: Seven Crises in Irish Criminal Justice*, Dublin: Round Hall, Sweet and Maxwell

O'Malley, T. (1996), *Sexual Offences*, Dublin: Round Hall, Sweet and Maxwell

Rottman, D.B. (1980), *Crime in the Republic of Ireland: Statistical Trends and Their Interpretation*, Dublin: The Economic and Social Research Institute

Rottman, D.B. (1984), *The Criminal Justice System: Policy and Performance*, Dublin: National Economic and Social Council

Smith, B.A. (1980), 'The Irish General Prisons Board, 1877–1885: Efficient Deterrence or Bureaucratic Ineptitude', *Irish Jurist*, vol. XV (New Series), 122–36

Vaughan, W.E. (1989), 'Ireland circa 1870' in W.E. Vaughan (ed.), *A New History of Ireland Volume V: Ireland under the Union, Volume 1, 1801–70*, Oxford: The Clarendon Press

Wilbanks, W. (1996), 'Homicide in Ireland', *International Journal of Comparative and Applied Criminal Justice*, vol. 20

OFFICIAL PUBLICATIONS

Department of Justice, Reports on Prisons and Places of Detention (1929–)

Department of Justice (1997), *Tackling Crime*

Department of Justice (1994), *The Management of Offenders: A Five Year Plan*

Garda Síochána, Annual Reports

Garda Síochána, Reports on Crime (1947–)

Judicial Statistics (1863–1921)

Law Reform Commission (1993), *Consultation Paper on Sentencing*

Law Reform Commission (1996), *Report on Sentencing*

Report of the Committee of Inquiry into the Penal System (1985)

Reports of the General Prison Board for Ireland (1878–1928)

Statistical Abstracts (1928–)

14

Europe and the Wider World

DERMOT MCALEESE[1]

Two statements can confidently be made about the Irish economy of the late 1990s. First, Ireland, according to all accepted international economic indicators, has become a wealthy country. Second, it has become more closely linked (in economics jargon: more integrated) in the European and the global economy than ever before. Some twenty-five years after Ireland joined the European Community, this is a good time to stand back and review the contribution of economic integration to the Irish economy. Have closer economic links with Europe and the wider world added to Ireland's prosperity? Will deepening this involvement – through the single market, through international agreements brokered through the World Trade Organisation, through expansion of the European Union to include Eastern Europe, and through economic and monetary union – consolidate our new-found prosperity? Or will it, as some fear, lead to more job insecurity, rootlessness and vulnerability to the ups and downs of the global economy? The evidence to date suggests that global free-trade in goods and services, and the opening of international capital markets will, on balance, improve the economic position of Irish people. But the gains from trade do not occur automatically, and there will be a continuing need for good economic management (McAleese, 1986; 1987).

How trade creates prosperity

Within the short span of forty years, Ireland has changed from being a relatively inward-oriented economy to one of the most open and trade-dependent economies in the world. In 1998, exports from Ireland are forecast to be about IR£48 billion, equivalent to 90 per cent of gross domestic product (GDP). As recently as 1994 the export/GDP ratio was 65 per cent, then considered a high figure, and in 1964 it was only 32 per cent (McAleese and Hayes, 1995). Imports have also grown rapidly, but less so than exports. They are expected to total about IR£40 billion in 1998. Like many countries, Ireland's trade growth has been driven primarily by two-way exchange of rather similar goods (intra-industry trade), much of it involving transactions between different branches of multinational firms (Brulhart and McAleese, 1995).

This two-way expansion of trade has brought several benefits to the economy. First, productivity of people employed in Irish manufacturing and agriculture has jumped ahead. Trade has enabled, and indeed forced, Irish business to become more specialised and efficient and to employ best practice techniques used by their foreign competitors. Second, the need to survive against stiff international competition in an open international market ensures that Irish business upgrades productivity by staying abreast of best international practice. Third, the Irish consumer has benefited through cheaper goods in the shops and the range of choice has been vastly extended. For example, the ability to import from literally the five continents means that goods such as clothing are available in our high streets at relatively cheap prices. One no longer needs to be rich to dress smartly.

Imports have brought one further important benefit: they have enabled Irish people to enjoy the fruits of technological innovation developed outside Ireland. Think of the personal computer. The cost of developing the computer has fallen almost entirely on wealthier countries, such as the United States. Because of foreign trade, the Irish PC-user can enjoy the latest technology at falling prices without incurring any of the huge development costs that others have had to incur. In general we can say that more open economies, like Ireland, have greater opportunities of benefiting from new ideas and techniques developed abroad than more closed economies. Economists have come to regard this as one of the most powerful reasons explaining why open economies have tended to outperform closed economies (International Monetary Fund, 1993).

Trade in services

The process of integration has extended far beyond free trade in goods. International trade in services has also been growing and currently accounts for one-quarter of total trade. Services trade includes tourism, transport, consultancy, financial and insurance activities. Entirely new service industries have appeared on the Irish scene, such as the International Financial Services Centre in Dublin, already employing over 3,000 people, and telemarketing. The growth in such activities can be explained in the first instance by advances in technology, which have reduced the cost of transport and communication between countries. Another factor has been the realisation that an efficient services sector is important for economic development and that such efficiency can best be assured by opening hitherto protected sectors to foreign competition. The European Commission has played a lead role in driving this message home and through a series of directives has forced several reluctant governments (including the Irish government) to remove restrictions on competition in transport, telecommunications, banking and insurance. As a result of such liberalisation, cost of inputs to Irish exporters has fallen, Irish industry has become more competitive and all sorts of new products and activities (the mobile phone for instance) have been spawned. Here is another advantage of openness, not mentioned in the textbooks.

Financial transfers

As part of the integration process, Ireland has benefited from financial transfers from the EU on an unprecedented scale. These transfers have taken two main forms: resources received from the various Structural Funds and financial supports from the Common Agricultural Policy. Net receipts from the EU have amounted to a staggering IR£12 billion since 1990 alone, equal to a free gift of IR£3,500 to every person in Ireland, with virtually no political strings attached. Few countries have ever received largesse on such a grand scale. The objective of the Structural Funds is to achieve economic convergence, i.e. convergence of living standards, so that the recipients can play a full and equal part in the progress of the European Union. The only obligation on the Irish government has been to spend the money in a manner agreed in advance with Brussels. Far from proving onerous or intrusive, this obligation is a considerable improvement in the way public sector investment is planned and monitored (Honohan, 1997).

Trade and foreign investment

Free trade and what is called the internationalisation of production often go hand in hand, and Irish experience is no exception to this rule. Subsidiaries of foreign multinationals account for one out of every two jobs in Irish manufacturing, and for 40 per cent of our total export earnings. The US influence has been particularly marked. Some 50,000 Irish people have found well-paying jobs in US subsidiaries in the manufacturing sector alone (Ruane and Görg, 1997). American subsidiaries are visible throughout the length and breadth of Ireland.

Foreign investors are attracted to Ireland for several reasons. First, they can use Ireland's secure access to the EU and other foreign markets as a platform from which to export to these markets. (The Irish market on its own is far too small to attract any significant volume of inward manufacturing investment.) Second, Ireland's well-educated, motivated and English-speaking workforce also encourages inward investment. Third, overseas investors have been attracted by Ireland's low corporate taxes. These and other advantages of the economy have been skilfully marketed by the IDA over many years (Kennedy, 1998). Recent experience shows that, as more investors come to Ireland, more tend to follow. Partly this is because of agglomeration economies – a few new firms cause infrastructure to be developed, which lowers costs for followers. Partly it arises because of informational economies. If Microsoft, for example, operates successfully in Ireland, that tells other potential investors that Ireland must be a good place to do business in.

Foreign investment, however, does not come cheaply. More countries than ever are trying to attract foreign investors, and for the right type of investment project Ireland must either pay the going rate or lose the project. Grants, subsidies and tax incentives totalling many millions had to be provided by the taxpayer. So far the balance between the gains and costs from foreign investment has rested in Ireland's favour. The Irish

Exchequer has certainly gained from their presence. In 1994, for instance, corporate tax receipts from IDA-supported companies totalled IR£440 million, while grants provided to them amounted to IR£73 million (IDA Annual Report, 1997).

With so much foreign industry in Ireland, it is not surprising that questions are regularly raised about the vulnerability of the Irish economy to changes in economic conditions abroad or simply to altered foreign sentiment about Ireland's attractiveness as an investment location. But such worries are misplaced. There is no evidence that foreign industry is more volatile than Irish-owned industry – because of its stronger resources, the opposite is more likely to be the case. Also, foreign investment engenders many positive spill-over effects on Irish-owned companies. Multinationals have helped small Irish firms to develop expertise as suppliers. They have also given job experience and training to a cohort of talented young people. In other instances, by taking over small Irish companies, they have provided a significant financial reward for the entrepreneurs who started these companies, and encouraged others to follow. While it is true to some extent that industry in Ireland suffers from the Wimbledon syndrome – too many international players and not enough local winners – the locals are fighting back.

Foreign investment has been a two-way process. While foreign firms invest in Ireland, Irish firms are investing overseas at an increasingly rapid rate. Most firms quoted in the Irish Stock Exchange have acquired substantial investment positions abroad. Irish multinationals, such as Smurfits, CRH, Kerry Foods, Glen Dimplex, Bank of Ireland and AIB, derive only a fraction of their profits from their Irish operations. Subsidiaries of Irish food companies supply 18 per cent of the UK liquid milk market, 30 per cent of the UK cheese market, and an estimated 55 per cent of the UK red meat market (*Irish Farmers Journal*, 27 December 1997). Unfortunately, we still await a comprehensive economic analysis of the effects of this surge in outward investment on the Irish economy. My guess is that such a study would show that overseas investment makes a positive contribution to the economy by enabling Irish companies to diversify risk, to learn first-hand from foreign business practice, and to escape the confines of the small Irish market.

A key development in recent years has been the growth of foreign investment in the services sector. The influx of major British multiples, such as Marks and Spencers, Dixons and Tesco, into the Irish market in recent years has had a huge impact on the Irish retail market, and further incursions from overseas are likely in hitherto 'closed' sectors, such as telecommunications and energy. Such investment receives no support from the Irish government because, in economic terms, they are less evidently advantageous than greenfield investment. Yet, by exposing the Irish market to more intense competition, it can bring significant economic gains to the Irish consumer. As integration continues, we can expect deeper penetration by overseas firms of our financial sector and, within the next decade, it is quite possible that Irish banks, building societies and insurance sectors will be entirely under foreign control. Already, most Irish shopping centres are mere replicas of those found in any British city. All this may make for greater efficiency and lower prices – but also for a rather duller, less distinctive and less economically independent Ireland. This is another aspect of the integration process that deserves further research.

Portfolio capital flows

As nations trade more intensively, capital moves with it. Banks help to finance foreign trade and, when major companies invest abroad, domestic banks tend to follow their customers and become international themselves – witness the proliferation of foreign banks in the wake of the multinational inflows into Ireland. Borrowing and lending in foreign currencies becomes increasingly easy for governments, firms and individuals.

While the Treaty of Rome involved a commitment to freedom of capital movements, little was done to implement this provision prior to the Single European Act of 1987. Indeed, only since the early 1990s has capital become fully mobile between Ireland and the outside world. The effects have been quite startling. Nowadays, the humblest Irish citizen can invest in equities and bonds from every part of the globe through a myriad of exotic investment funds. Irish pension funds have increased their overseas holdings to over 40 per cent of their total assets of IR£19 billion, and the process of international diversification of Irish investment funds follows apace. The

Irish government's debt agency, the NTMA, scours the world market for the cheapest source of funds. Transactions between companies involve huge flows of money in and out of Ireland. Irish banks too are heavily involved in the global capital market – by mid-1997 their gross liabilities to non-residents amounted to IR£50 billion.

The abolition of capital controls means that Irish capital is free to go to where it can make the highest return and diversify risk. This freedom to borrow and lend abroad has brought economic benefits to Irish individuals and Irish companies by enabling them to diversify their portfolios and maximise the return on capital. It has also helped to ensure that the government keeps its finances in good order. Any hint of reversion to the irresponsible fiscal policies of the past would lead to prompt capital outflows, higher interest rates for Irish borrowers, and a very clear negative signal to the public about the government's performance. As an Italian economist once remarked, 'capital markets have the heart of a lamb, the legs of a hare, and the memory of an elephant'. Another benefit of capital mobility stems from its stabilising role in the economy. When the Irish economy is booming, profits flow out of Ireland to the outside world. When the rest of the world is booming and Irish economy is relatively depressed, profits from capital invested abroad flow in, domestic activity is bolstered by increased income. Thus, Irish consumers find their spending evened out over the business cycle (Lane, 1998).

A less edifying effect of international capital movement has been to make individual capital transactions increasingly difficult to trace and tax. The byzantine financial paths described in the 1997 report of the McCracken tribunal illustrated the difficulty in a graphic way. As a result, tax evasion and avoidance of taxation have become easier than before. Governments in high tax jurisdictions are therefore under pressure to reduce tax rates so as to minimise the incentives to transfer capital to lower tax jurisdictions. The danger of a resultant 'race to the bottom', or fiscal degradation, has caused concern in the European Union, and initiatives are in progress to secure closer co-ordination of capital taxation policies among member states. Globalisation of the private sector, in other words, must be matched by globalisation of public policy.

From emigration to immigration

No description of Ireland's integration with the outside world would be complete without reference to the movement of people, or in economic jargon: labour mobility. For most of the past two centuries, migration meant outward movement, or emigration. There is continuing debate about the effects of emigration on the economies to which the Irish emigrated, on the living standards of emigrants and, most controversial of all, on the living standards of those left behind. Emigration can certainly generate some positive effects in the short run, such as a reduction in the level of unemployment and a mitigation of the decline in living standards during recessions. The longer run effects are more difficult to quantify. But such evidence as exists offers no compelling support for the commonly-held view that emigration has impaired the long-run development of the economy, or the growth of income per person (NESC, 1991).

Movements of people, like movements of capital, can go both ways. As the Irish economy has grown in prosperity, it has become a magnet for returning Irish emigrants, for skilled Europeans willing to work in the computer and teleservices industries, and also for large numbers of relatively unskilled people from poorer nations. Increasingly one sees advertisements for jobs in Dublin bars and restaurants specifying that 'fluency in English is essential'.

Being a recipient, rather than a source, of surplus labour has proven a disturbingly novel experience for Ireland in recent years. The phenomenon is too recent to enable any proper assessment of its economic impact. We can safely assert that inflows of skilled people, many of them returning emigrants, are beneficial to the economy. However, the economic calculus becomes less clear when it comes to judging the value of immigrants who are unskilled, yet ready and eager to work. First, Ireland has an abundance of unskilled people already, languishing in unemployment, and it is reasonable to give them priority ahead of economic immigrants (political refugees are, of course, another matter). Second, we must ensure that unskilled immigrants find work, which will enable them to make the same positive contribution to society as generations of Irish have done in Britain and the United States. Were they to lapse into welfare dependency and long-term unemployment, we would lose and so would they in the long run.

As a general rule, economics suggests that moving capital, technology and goods between countries is likely to be less costly and disruptive in social terms than moving people. As the slogan goes, jobs should go to people rather than people to jobs. But when jobs won't move, people of ambition have no choice but to up and go themselves.

EMU – the next step

The next step in the integration process is the introduction of a single currency, the euro, and economic and monetary union (EMU). The surrender of the Irish pound and its replacement by the euro is proving to be a difficult and controversial step.

It is a difficult step because introducing a new currency will be a costly nuisance for every single individual and every single business in the country. By the year 2002, all prices will have to be quoted in euros. Automatic teller machines and accounting systems will have to be adjusted to transactions in euros. The cost of this has been estimated at several hundred million pounds. And it will have to be borne by the private sector and ultimately, one suspects, by ordinary consumers – Brussels has made clear that it will not foot the bill. Also, for individuals, calculating the euro equivalent of Irish pounds will be troublesome. The transition process will create opportunities for confusion, fraud and unwarranted price increases as uneven and awkward figures are rounded up. Economists tend to see these costs as similar to the upfront costs of launching a new product, which should be capitalised and written off against a future stream of benefits lasting for many generations.

This brings us to the controversial side of EMU. The controversy about Ireland's participation in EMU is intriguing in two respects. First, it has divided Irish economists to a degree that no other European initiative has done since membership of the European Community was proposed in the late 1950s. Second, opponents of EMU entry seem to have been uniquely ineffective in changing policy makers' minds. Ireland's main policy makers political parties, business representatives and trade unions remain as firmly pro-EMU as ever. Fascinating material here surely for future economists and political scientists!

There are two standard economic benefits to Ireland of EMU. First, trade and foreign investment with the eleven member states in EMU will be easier and less expensive to transact in a single currency with zero exchange rate risk. Second, the euro will make it easier for people to compare prices in different parts of Europe. Price transparency will ensure that competition is intensified and prices are kept low.

Against this are ranged two main drawbacks.[2] One derives from Irish firms' vulnerability to changes in sterling, given that Britain has decided to opt out of EMU. Business was badly scarred by the weakness of sterling in 1992–93 and also in 1986, and many firms had extreme difficulty in coping with a rate of one Irish pound equal to 110p sterling. Had the single currency been in operation in 1992, Irish firms would have had to cope with the equivalent of 115–120p sterling per Irish pound through much of 1995 and 1996. In recent times, sterling has strengthened, but the possibility of it weakening again cannot be ruled out.

Another objection to EMU is that it will result in inappropriate interest rates for the Irish economy. A booming economy ideally needs higher interest rates to cool things down. But, after EMU, the Irish Central Bank will surrender control of monetary policy to the European Central Bank. Interest rates will be determined by the needs of the European, not the Irish, economy. While all members of EMU will be in the same position in this respect, the Irish economy has been weakly synchronised with average EU economic conditions in the past and hence, the argument goes, conflict is likely to arise often in the future. Thus, when we need high interest rates, we are likely to get lower rates, and vice versa.

While there would be general agreement that going into EMU has potential downsides, opponents of EMU tend to underplay the equally serious downsides of staying out.

First, there is the risk that foreign investors would be put off by what would be perceived as a weakening commitment to Europe and a danger, however remote and ill-defined, that Ireland might suffer from not being close to the centre of decision-taking in European monetary policy. The IDA claims that failure to participate in EMU would have a serious adverse effect on inward investment.

Second, abstention from EMU might weaken the government's commitment to fiscal control and a lower debt/GDP ratio. Were this to happen, failure to join EMU would be regarded by future generations as a truly calamitous decision. It is worth keeping in mind that, without the disciplining effect of the Maastricht criteria on Irish fiscal policy, the present economic boom would never have happened. Our present prosperity and competitive exchange rate are the consequence of the government's commitment to participate in EMU. They are connected phenomena. This is the basic flaw in the 'if it ain't broke, don't fix it' argument for staying out of EMU.

Third, the picture promoted by critics of EMU of a high-octane Irish Central Bank, fine tuning the economy from year to year and providing soft landings or quick recoveries à la carte, is not entirely plausible. This strand in the anti-EMU case relies on an exaggerated faith in the effectiveness of counter-cyclical monetary policy. The Federal Reserve Bank in the United States, of course, operates such a system quite successfully. But for a small open country it is a different matter. The problem is that adjusting interest rates according to the cyclical pattern of the economy can generate large, and often uncontrollable, swings in the exchange rate. Businesses in these countries generally dislike exchange rate volatility and uncertainty, which explains why companies tend to favour the EMU project (Britain and Sweden not excepted). Studies of the economics of introducing a flexible exchange rate regime in Ireland have concluded that the exchange rate uncertainty of such a regime would impose excessive costs on our trade and foreign investment.

Some critics of EMU recommend that the Central Bank should focus on an effective exchange rate target for the Irish pound, thus steering a middle course between fluctuations in sterling and the euro. But the closer the Central Bank sticks to the middle course in exchange rate policy, the more circumscribed its power to alter interest rates and implement strong counter-cyclical monetary policies.

A curious aspect of the EMU debate in Ireland is that while opponents criticise it on the grounds that it will be bad for Irish business, Irish business itself has generally been strongly supportive of the government's position.[3] So also has the Irish voter. There is, for example, the plain fact that the Maastricht referendum in 1992 recorded a 'yes' vote of just under 70 per cent of all votes cast. Some opponents of EMU brush this result aside on the basis that the Irish people did not know what they were voting for. Fortunately for democracy, our politicians and civil servants are unable to dismiss a referendum vote so lightly. Besides, why were the people not informed of the downsides? Criticisms of the Irish government's strategy towards EMU have come too late. In retrospect, it is a pity that these valid and important criticisms were not fully debated, and alternative strategies proposed, prior to, rather than after, the 1992 referendum.

A further consideration is that Structural Funds, especially those received during the 1990s, were designed to assist Ireland in its professed objective of building up its economic strength and participating fully in EMU. Having received, and spent, this assistance, and subsequently prospered and passed the Maastricht criteria with flying colours, could an Irish government credibly declare that it had changed its mind and had decided not to join, until the UK joins too? After all the sterling factor and the 'asymmetric shocks' problem have not hit us out of the blue. More important, would such a policy reversal not go against the whole thrust of Irish political economy over the past thirty years, which has been to lessen our economic dependence on Britain and establish an independent role on a broader international stage?

To summarise, the ineffectiveness of the anti-EMU case can be traced to three main defects. One relates to timing – the anti-arguments have come too late in the decision-making process. Another defect relates to content – the arguments are substantive, but not compelling. A final problem concerns perspective – a decision to go into or stay out of EMU should not be dictated by short-term considerations, whether they be the specific sterling exchange rate in any month or the existence or absence of a housing boom in Dublin. Even if a convincing case on economic grounds could be made for staying out of EMU, such a policy reversal would require the articulation of an alternative strategy for Ireland's long-term development, not just a simple 'no'.

Hence, Ireland is ineluctably drawn towards early participation in the single currency. Over the long run, EMU could result in a consolidation of the benefits of fiscal consolidation, low inflation and fast growth experienced in recent years. But we are speaking of probabilities, not certainties. Much will depend on how the levers of domestic policy on, for instance, incomes, education, infrastructure and tax, still left to us are deployed. If the UK stays out of EMU and sterling behaves with as much volatility as in the past, Irish businesses and employees (and their trade unions) will have to be prepared to respond far more flexibly than in the past. For Ireland, the question now is not whether, but how, to adapt to the new disciplines and opportunities which EMU will impose.

Conclusions

Two key global trends in recent years have been (1) the liberalisation of economies to give greater scope to market forces, and (2) the globalisation of markets. The growing importance of European integration for the Irish economy is the mirror image of processes affecting many other countries throughout the world. The scope of Ireland's integration, not just with Europe but with overseas markets generally, has grown at an extraordinary pace. The next step after EMU will be the further enlargement of the EU, from its present fifteen members to twenty, to include the more developed East European countries. Not long after that an EU of twenty-six members is on the cards. By then, the EU will have become a truly major economic power, and Ireland will increasingly have assumed the features of a tiny regional economy of the EU.

As a regional economy of a vastly enlarged and more market-driven EU, Ireland will have to survive without many of the supports it has enjoyed over the past twenty-five years. Structural Funds are in the process of being phased out, following our graduation into the higher income league. The days of large inflows to our farmers through the Common Agricultural Policy are likewise numbered. If things go wrong, fiscal policy will be severely circumscribed and there will be no friendly and familiar Irish Central Bank to adjust interest rates suited to our needs. In this regard, it is vitally important that Ireland should be allowed to maintain its favorable corporation tax regime. At present, the government has proposed altering the 10 per cent corporations profits tax to a general rate of 12.5 per cent applicable to all businesses. This proposal is currently under scrutiny in Brussels.

Integration in the European economy needs to be managed correctly. There is no evidence that jobs in an integrated economy are less secure than in a protected one. Also, as experience over the past twenty-five years has demonstrated, while exposure to overseas markets has made the Irish economy more vulnerable to external fluctuations, the trade-off has been improvements in living standards, health and education, which more than compensate. True, the penalty for policy mistakes is likely to increase as a result of integration. But provided such mistakes are avoided, further improvements in living standards are certainly likely. Greater access to knowledge and technology, the stimulus of competition with world-class rivals, the resource allocation gains from being able to trade at world prices and better access to the global pool of saving – these will remain the core sources of economic growth (McAleese, 1997).

Economic forces are notoriously two-handed. For every opportunity there is a challenge; and few economic changes leave everyone a winner. Continued growth for the Irish economy will depend on the ability of firms in Ireland to grasp the opportunities, and on the ability of Irish policymakers to make Ireland an attractive location for export business.

NOTES

1 The author is grateful to Holger Görg, Kieran Kennedy, Philip Lane, Vivienne Ryan and Eric Strobl for helpful comments

2 The case against Ireland joining EMU is made in Thom (1997), Thom and Neary (1997) and Neary (1997). It is worth noting that those articulating the case are by no means anti-European in the colloquial sense of that term. Some, like Neary, happily describe themselves as Europhiles, but with a capital E of course

3 Ireland's main business and employer organisation, IBEC, has been a proactive and unequivocal supporter of participation in EMU in the first round. Small business organisations have been more tentative

REFERENCES

Brulhart, M. and McAleese, D. (1995), 'Intra-Industry Trade and Industrial Adjustment: the Irish Experience', *Economic and Social Review*, January 1995, pp. 107–129

Honohan, P. (ed.) (1997), *CSF Mid-term Evaluation*, Final Report prepared for the Department of Finance by the Economic and Social Research Institute in association with Peter Bacon and Associates, DKM Economic Consultants and Brendan Kearney and Associates

International Monetary Fund (1993), 'Trade as an Engine of Growth', *World Economic Outlook*, May

Kennedy, K.A. (1998), 'Industrial Development', Thomas Davis lecture (this series)

Lane, P.R. (1998), 'International Diversification and the Irish Economy', Trinity Economic Papers, Technical Paper no. 98/11

McAleese, D. (1997), *Economics for Business*, London: Prentice Hall

McAleese, D. (1987), 'European Integration and the Irish Economy', *Administration*, vol. 35, no. 2, Dublin: Institute of Public Administration

McAleese, D. (1986), 'Ireland in the World Economy', in K.A. Kennedy (ed.) *Ireland in Transition*, Mercier Press

McAleese, D. and Hayes, F. (1995), 'European Integration the Balance of Payments and Inflation', in J. O'Hagan, *The Economy of Ireland*, London: Macmillan

Neary, J.P. and Thom, D.R. (forthcoming), 'Punts, pounds and euros: In search of an optimum currency area', in *IBAR – Journal of Irish Business Administration and Research*

Neary, J.P. (1997), 'The EU Stability Pact and the Case for European Monetary Union', Centre for Economic Research Working Paper 97/28, Dublin: University College Dublin

NESC (1991), *The Economic and Social Implications of Emigration*, Dublin

Ruane, F. and Görg, H. (1997), 'The Impact of Foreign Direct Investment on Sectoral Adjustment in the Irish Economy', *National Institute Economic Review*, April

Thom, D.R. (1997), 'Economic and Monetary Union', Centre for Economic Research Working Paper 97/3, January, Dublin: University College Dublin